The Football Coaches' Guide to Clock Management

John Sterner

ISBN: 1-58518-775-5
Library of Congress Control Number: 2002116285

Book layout: Jennifer Bokelmann
Cover design: Kerry Hartjen
Front cover photo: Tom Hauck/Allsport

Coaches Choice
P.O. Box 1828
Monterey, CA 93942
www.coacheschoice.com

Dedication

To Sue for helping me pursue those things that I love. To Keeley and Jack for cheering no matter what the score, "Go Dad, go Muskego!"

Acknowledgments

Thanks to Stan Zweifel for encouraging me to write this book and for his endless dedication to the betterment of football. Thanks Clay Iverson, Dennis Johnson and Bob LeBoeuf for their assistance. I also want to extend my appreciation to Gary Grzesk for his thoughts on some of the basketball perspectives discussed in this book. And, thanks to David Stephens and Ashley Kiefer for their assistance in compiling the data. Finally, I would also thank Bob LeBoeuf, an assistant on our staff, whose ambition, diligence and observations have made him a valuable sounding board for me.

Preface

When I first began coaching football I had some idea about what clock management had to do with winning football games. Although, I thought I had a good idea of how important it was, I was ignorant to the weight and scope of clock management as a tool for winning more games. Yes, I was aware of the fact that the two-minute drill was an important part of the end-of-the-half and end-of-the-game strategy, and I also knew that running the ball allowed you to lengthen the time of possession, kill the clock when ahead late in the game, and give the defense some advantages. However, that was basically the extent of it.

In 1994, after listening to Stan Zweifel, then and now the offensive coordinator at UW-Whitewater, talk about the topic of clock management and some of its applications, I realized that there was more to it than that. As I moved in and out of various high school jobs, my fascination and appreciation of the depth and breadth of the topic grew steadily stronger. In 1998, as a freshman assistant coach at Muskego High School in Wisconsin, where I am currently the head coach, I began to experiment with all-game clock management with the freshman team. This step was a significant leap from where I had begun, and it opened up many doors for our team, as our freshman "A" and "B" teams both went undefeated, posting a 12-0 combined record.

In the off-season of that same year, the year I also became the head coach at Muskego, I read a book called *Football Clock Management* by John T. Reed, which opened up even more possibilities for our team's success, relative to clock management. Since 1998 my philosophy has grown apart from Reed's in very distinct ways and has become a contradiction to much of his.

While it is likely that I would have never developed our teams "dictated tempo" philosophy into what it is today without the contributions of these two coaches, it is a departure, to be sure, from the clock-management philosophy I have seen or read elsewhere. Because so little has ever been written about football clock management, my departures from "conventional" wisdom have come through trial and error, a study of statistics, and being able to bounce ideas off other coaches.

Contents

Introduction

THE OBJECT OF THE GAME IS TO WIN! This goal is the bottom line. As such, barring anything that would be considered unethical, you, as a coach, should do everything in your power to put your team in the best position to do so. A number of coaches exist who would certainly give lip service to this idea. On the other hand, many individuals apparently are not willing to do the little things to get there. This circumstance is true, not just in sport, but in life—it is certainly the factor that frequently distinguishes those who are successful from those who are not. What causes such an aversion to attempting to achieve success? While the possible answers to this question are many and varied, the responses may be narrowed down to two broad categories: #1) some individuals are too lazy to do the little things, while #2) other people are afraid to do what is necessary.

Football is no different. For example, if you are reading this book, let's presume that you have enough ambition to disqualify yourself from category "#1". Chances are you may be in category "#2" and afraid of some the steps required in learning how to properly manage the clock.

Fear is an extremely strong motivator in the game of football. Some coaches may fear the time it takes to initiate and install new tactics. In this regard, others may fear the opinions of players, parents, fans, fellow coaches, administrators, alumni and media. Although it may be the first instinct of a coach, who is filled with fear and bravado to dismiss something new, different, or un-orthodox, it will definitely improve your chances of winning football games.

In fact, proper clock management involves many aspects that buck conventional wisdom that are ignored by coaches in an effort to quell their fears. On the other hand, if you buy into the concepts and techniques involved in proper clock management, they will reward you many times over.

All coaches are looking for that "secret formula" that will give them an extra edge and allow them to win more games. In this regard, this book is designed to give you a significant edge by showing you how to properly manage the clock. And, make no mistake about it, doing so will help your team win more football games—this is an indisputable fact.

All coaches concur that winning is about doing the little things. They demand it of their players. The point to keep in mind is that regardless of your team's offense or defense, strengths or deficiencies, properly managing the clock will improve your team's chances of winning. Accordingly, it is now up to you to do the "little things" and learn how to properly manage the clock. In the process, you will help your team win more football games.

CHAPTER 1

A Basketball Perspective of Clock Management

My first recollection of having an interest in clock management came as a kid watching basketball. I grew up watching some of the basketball coaches who helped bring clock management to prominence in their sport. Being a native of the Milwaukee area at a time—when the Marquette Warriors were among the top teams in country in the 1970's, I can recall watching Al McGuire manipulate the clock. The broadcasters and fans were very aware of his "deliberate-pace" tactics, and at times, this approach was unpopular. However, Coach McGuire is currently remembered for the success that he achieved in his career that made him one of America's most beloved coaches.

McGuire was popular for many reasons, among those that he was a good person. Realistically, however, he was popular because he won basketball games. People don't generally tend to remember his deliberate game pace. Everyone loves a winner. It is sometimes amazing what people choose to remember about an individual or a particular event.

McGuire's success was undoubtedly due, in no small part, to his knowledge that properly using the clock would give his teams a distinct advantage over his opponent. In fact, many other basketball coaches, such as former North Carolina coach Dean Smith, with his "four-corners" offense and Dick Bennett, former head men's basketball coach at Wisconsin, have regularly been recognized for and benefited from their clock-management tactics. In the sport of football, however, this situation has never really been the case. A football coach is rarely recognized for his tactical ability involving pace. Is it possible that the factor of pace could be so lopsidedly important in one game that involves use of a play clock and not another? Hardly. In reality, sound clock management is just as important in football. The majority of the football world, however, including the fans and media, has not yet embraced these virtues.

The point that needs to be emphasized is that football coaches (or any coaches whose sport uses a clock for that matter) should be using the clock to help win games. Doing so can dramatically impact the outcome of the game. This approach has occurred in basketball. In fact, at one time, manipulating the clock gave some teams in basketball such an advantage that the rules had to be changed. As a result, the shot clock, which limits a team's stalling strategy, was instituted. Note that it limits a team's stalling strategy, it does not eliminate it. In fact, most college and pro basketball coaches still consider "pace" an important component of their strategy, in spite of the fact that a shot clock is used. In high school, teams can still take advantage of all-out stalling, one might conclude, because the cost of shot clock equipment is prohibitive.

If clock management can be used to give a team an edge in basketball, many of the principles attendant to sound clock management can apply just as easily to football. Football, after all, has a shot clock of sorts with its "play clock". However, the overwhelming majority of football coaches don't consider clock management an important enough factor to pay attention to until the last few minutes of the half or the game.

Why not use the "shot clock" in football to your advantage? When viewed in comparison to basketball, football actually has an advantage over college and pro basketball, because in football, you can determine exactly when you want to "take the shot" by snapping the ball exactly when you deem it appropriate. As a football coach, you could opt to snap the ball with only one second having elapsed off the play clock, or with only one second remaining. In basketball, because you are somewhat limited by the quality of the shot selection, which may require you to take a shot sooner or later than you would have ideally planned to, this approach is not realistic.

With the common sense and exceptional success basketball coaches have demonstrated over the years in applying clock management strategies to their game plans, it would seem long past due that football coaches begin stepping in line. Relatively speaking, football coaches are in the stone age compared to their basketball counterparts when it comes to clock management. As will become even more apparent in the chapters that follow this one, there are far too many advantages to managing the clock for football coaches to ignore this facet of the game any longer.

CHAPTER 2

When to Manage the Clock

With regard to clock management, a number of myths and misunderstandings exist. One of the first notions that needs to be dispelled is that clock management should be relegated to special situations, such as the two-minute and four-minute drills. Clock management is an all-game endeavor. Your team will almost always benefit from conserving or wasting the clock, because your team will almost always be either a favorite or an underdog. Keep in mind that being a favorite or an underdog does not just refer to the pre-game setting. In the middle of the game, as well, you should also have an indication of who is most likely to win the game.

The second notion that should be dispelled is that clock-management is an offensive tactic. While it is true that you generally have more control of the clock when your team is on offense, with the exception of your opponent's ability to use timeouts, there are a number of clock-management tactics you can use on defense and special teams as well. Clock management is not just all-game; it is also all-phase. Marrying the three phases (offense, defense and special teams) of your team into one mutually beneficial philosophy will go a long way toward ensuring that you are not "robbing Peter, to pay Paul," by having one phase of your game wasting time and another phase of your game conserving time.

Keep in mind the reference to the fact that you should "almost" always manage the clock. This is because you will sometimes be in a position where you are evenly matched with your opponent, and the likelihood of either team winning appears to be even. The perception of your team as favorite or underdog is based upon your professional opinion, as a coach, and it is not static. From pre-game through the final tick of the clock, you are the individual who is most qualified to assess the dynamic element of your team's ever-changing probability of winning the game. You are the person who has spent the most time breaking down film and analyzing your team's tendencies, strengths, and weaknesses. As such, you are the individual who is most capable of assessing your team's chances of winning at any point along the way, hopefully, without undue bias. Doing so "without bias" is critical in being able to properly employ the clock management strategy that is needed to win the game.

The aforementioned factor has nothing to do with being optimistic or pessimistic. It refers to the fact that, given all of the information that you have concerning the probable outcome of the game at any point in the game, you can employ the proper strategy. Some of this information will certainly come in the form of momentum and emotion, but much of it will also be based on more tangible evidence gained from pre-game and in-game information, such as tendencies, current field position, the number of timeouts remaining, and a myriad of other types of information. Your professional appraisal of the marriage of tangible and intangible evidence will be the best indicator of what mode of clock management your team should be in. The cogent point to remember is that you need to be conscious of, and at almost all times employing, some type of clock management. The only time to not manage the clock is when there is no clear favorite or clear underdog. Choosing to not manage the clock can spell disaster. To paraphrase one of our former Presidents, "Above all else, do something."

CHAPTER 3

Determining Your Team's Tempo to Open the Game

In order to determine the tempo you want to use to open the game, you must make an educated guess as to who is likely to win the game and by how much. This subjective calculation should be done, imagining that neither team will pay much attention to all-game clock management. In other words, if you were another coach analyzing your game, whom would you predict as the favorite and what kind of point spread would you assign?

Often times, we do this on our own staff, (i.e., predict the favorite and the point spread of other games in our conference that week). While this process is certainly entertaining, it serves a much more valuable purpose in learning how to handicap a game, so that when it comes time we have had practice in handicapping our own games. This undertaking of course has nothing to do with wagering money, but rather with the exercise of determining a likely winner. If you try this with your own staff, you will probably find that the process has mixed results, particularly with the point-spreads. If it was easy to do, there would be a lot of coaches who would switch their occupations to something located near Las Vegas, Reno, or Atlantic City.

On the other hand, what would happen if you asked your staff to pick just two winners for the week in conference play? You can bet that they would be more successful in these predictions, than they would in determining accurate spreads, or even just the winners of each game. You can also bet that the lower you go in competition levels, the more success you would have in predicting the outcomes of games. Your predictive insights would be enhanced because the lower you go in competition levels, from NFL to NCAA, and from NCAA to high school, the greater disparity in skill level from one team to the next. As a result, a greater number of lopsided victories will occur. In other words, a greater margin of victory as you go lower in levels will exist. The point to keep in mind is that being able to accurately assess your own team's win probability at any time from the pre-game to the final seconds of the game will have a definite impact on your ability to put your team in the proper clock-management mode.

The importance of being able to predict a winner has its roots in some compelling statistics. In researching 322 regular season games in the state of Wisconsin during the 2001 season, there were some very telling statistics, that will be referred to throughout the book. The study found that 267 times, or 82.9% of the time, the team who scored first went on to win the game. In 1999, I had done the same study and found that 80.5% of 262 games were won by the team who scored first.

Another research effort determined the percentage of times that the team who scored first went on to win by a blowout, (a term that is somewhat arbitrarily determined to be a victory by 28 points or more, given the fact that a 28-point lead at any point in the game, although it has been overcome on very infrequent occasions, is virtually insurmountable). The statistics indicated that the team who scored first went on to win by a blowout a whopping 41.6% of the time, or 111 times out of 267. Yet another study was somewhat similar, and measured the total number of blowouts, regardless of whether or not a team had scored first. This scenario happened 132 out of 322 times, or 41% of the time. Chart 3-1 illustrates the aforementioned statistics.

Chart 3-1. Likelihood of winning and winning by a blowout statistics	
First team scoring wins the game:	80.5-82.9%
First team scoring wins the game by blowout:	41.6%
Either team wins by blowout:	41.0%

If, as a coach, you can accurately assess your team's chances of winning or losing and the expected point difference, you will be able to more successfully determine what mode of clock management your team should be in. Prior to the game, you should be able to assign your team to one of five categories:

- Category #1 – a blowout favorite (≥ 28 points)
- Category #2 – a favorite (8-27 points)
- Category #3 – slight favorite or slight underdog (+/– 7 points)
- Category #4 – an underdog (8-27 points)
- Category #5 – a blowout underdog (≥ 28 points)

If these categories seem somewhat inexact, that is appropriate. After all, at best, the process is an inexact science, and if everyone knew the outcome, no need would exist to play the game. On the other hand, making a professionally educated assessment of the outcome can give your team an increased chance of winning the game. The key point in this regard is keep in mind that an "increased chance" does not equal a "guaranteed chance," because nothing is written in stone. Let's face it, if your team is a blowout favorite, even screwing a few things up will probably not sink you. Conversely, if your team is a blowout underdog, a few breaks will probably not float your boat, but it will increase your chances and give you a better-case-scenario for achieving success, than if you hadn't managed the clock at all.

It is critical for you to be able to determine into which category your team fits. This factor is particularly crucial when distinguishing between categories #1 and #3, and categories #3 and #5. Being able to do so, gives your team the best chance for being able to take advantage of what could be termed "the fluke". One possible way to understand how to take advantage of the fluke is to think of a coin-flip metaphor.

For example, imagine that you are going to play a fictitious game called the weighted-coin-flip game. It is different from other coin-flips, because you know beforehand that one side is intentionally unequally weighted. The "heads" side is weighted so that it is 20 times more likely to come up than the "tails" side. Next, you are told that you are not going to have a choice as to which side to call. Instead, you are going to be assigned one side of the coin. This set of circumstances doesn't seem fair does it? But, this scenario is akin to being on a team that is either the blowout favorite or the blowout underdog. You don't get to change sides before the game. You have to do the best you can with the side you have to improve your chances of winning. In this fictitious game, the variable that you are given, however, is that once you know which side you've been assigned to you will get to determine how many times the coin is going to be flipped. You can choose either two flips of the coin or 200; you need to choose the one option that will give you the best chance of winning.

If you are assigned the heads side (the blowout favorite), and you are smart, you should opt for 200 flips of the coin. In doing so, you have assured yourself that, by the end of the game, the score is going to be roughly "heads team" 190 and "tails team" 10. Because you have chosen the higher number of flips, you will have virtually eliminated any chance for the "tails team" to have some kind of "fluke" victory.

On the other hand, if you are assigned to the tails side (the underdog), you should opt for two flips of the coin. Choosing this option will not guarantee a victory. In fact, chances are that you will still lose. However, after the first flip, the score will presumably be "heads team" 1, "tails team" 0. This situation is a much more inviting scenario for you, as the coach of the "tails team," because at halftime you are still in the game. One more flip of the coin could give you a stunning upset. The prospect of this type of performance can thrill you, cause your adrenaline level to increase, fill you with hope, and provide you with momentum.

In reality, you will still probably lose, even with the score at 1 to 0, but probability tells you the best chance to win or tie the game will come within the first two flips. Consequent flips will only serve to widen the scoring gap.

But football ain't coin-flippin'. Unlike coin flipping, emotion can and does play a part in determining the outcome of football games. If your team was down 1-0 in football game against a blowout favorite with one-flip left, how pumped up do you suppose your team would be? A hell of a lot more than if the score was 190 to 9. So the virtue of your managing the number of flips had a synergistic effect. Not only is the score closer, but because the prospect of your team winning is greater, emotion and momentum have become factors as well.

The prospect of an upset, undoubtedly, would be having an affect on the "heads team" as well, which by now would be paralyzed with disbelief, doubting their abilities, having had their confidence shaken. At this point, synergism would have taken a negative toll on the "heads team." They would be suffering from the same syndrome as a famous little bird that incorrectly and frantically exclaimed, "The sky is falling." On the "heads team" sideline the sky *IS* falling. The little bird didn't know that it was merely an acorn that hit him on the head, and that if he would have listened to sound advice, he would not have run into the street and been killed. He chose to ignore reason. He chose to panic, and his *panic* was his own undoing. What would the "heads team" members have said if they had known that their coach was given pre-game advice to increase the number of flips, and the coach chose to ignore it? Possibly, oh, what a dumb-dumb Chicken Little!

In fact, this scenario is typically seen when many coaches initially attempt to employ any clock management strategy in the game—Chicken Little-style. It usually happens in the final minutes of a game and is performed in concert with a frantic and dramatic shift of gears. Because the tempo that the team had been operating in was much slower and is now so suddenly and decidedly faster, the team experiences a psychological whiplash. This factor is usually the result when a coach carelessly disregards any clock-management strategy up to that point in the game. Furthermore, whatever clock-management strategy a coach ultimately adopts may not have been practiced in such a way as to promote a calm demeanor among the players. As a result, "the sky is falling" because of the coach's own disregard for prior sound reasoning. While this situation can usually be prevented, the current set of circumstances, coupled with the players' state of panic, will inevitably often spell defeat.

CHAPTER 4

Reasons to Slowdown or Kill the Clock

Several situations exist where you should try to keep the clock running, shorten the game, and give yourself an advantage over your opponent. Some of these reasons may be solely powerful enough to cause you to want to kill the clock, while others must be weighed against or considered in concert with other criteria. Among the most plausible reasons to consider killing the clock are the following:

☐ **When going into a game and you perceive your team to be an underdog or a blowout underdog, you should be wasting time for most of the game.** This suggestion goes directly against the recommendation of some pundits who say you should be in a full-speed hurry-up when you are an underdog or losing. These individuals contend that since the majority of the time (80+% depending on the year and the league surveyed) the team that is ahead is going to win, the team that is losing should be conserving time and operating as quickly as possible, in order to get more possessions and climb back into the game. While this well-intentioned advice would appear to be true, upon closer inspection, hurrying-up when you are a blowout underdog might be the worst thing you could do.

In order to properly consider this factor, you should refer back to the statistics from Chapter 3 that indicated that the team who scores first goes on to win 82.9% of the time. This finding is very similar to the NFL statistics that have been reported. However, when a team is a blowout underdog, which is 41% of the time, giving yourself and your opponent more possessions by being in a full-speed, hurry-up mode will only accentuate your opponent's strengths and your relative weaknesses. It is the equivalent of the weaker "tails team," discussed in the previous chapter, electing to flip the coin 200 times instead of two times. While more possessions for you will certainly improve the chances that you will score, it will also improve the chance that your stronger opponent will not only score, but will do so with greater frequency than you.

I once had a telephone conversation with a person about clock-management strategy for football coaches who mentioned that he once had made a suggestion to a coach at a nearby area high school, who was facing an opponent with a very impressive winning streak. The coach of the team with whom this individual was speaking did not have a very strong team that year and was definitely a blowout underdog. As such, the recommendation that this person made to the coach was that he go into a slowdown, whereby he should attempt to keep the possessions to an absolute minimum, in an effort to keep the score close and win by "fluke" at the end of the game. At the time, it sounded like a very good idea to me. In fact, it is much of the same thought philosophy that is espoused in this book.

Subsequently, when I e-mailed the person who had made the suggestion to the coach with the weighted coin-flip analogy being analogous to a game with a blowout scenario, he dismissed my notion as not being based on statistics. At the time, I supposed he was right, in that the weighted coin-flip metaphor was, perhaps, based more on probability (theory) than statistics (reality). As a result, I decided to conduct some statistically based research on blowouts.

Some individuals claim that wasting time as an underdog is tantamount to coaching malpractice, because the team who is winning will eventually win 82.9% of the time. Contrary to these would-be sages, however, you *DO* need to conserve the clock, because there is an 80.5 to 82.9% chance you will lose anyhow. In 41.6% of those instances when you are trailing, you are not only going to get beat, but you are going to get blown-out by 28 points or more. As such, you would be in a mode of operation that is the least conducive to success, between 58.7% and 61.1% of the time. In other words, being in a hurry-up mode when trailing, as the would–be sages suggest, rather than a slowdown mode, would increase your chances of losing. This conclusion is based upon the fact that as either an underdog or a blowout underdog only 17.1-19.5% of the time when your opponent scores first will you come back and win, plus the 41.6% of the time that you will get blown out, that you would have been in the wrong mode, (a hurry-up mode) of clock management for a total of 58.7 to 61.1% of the time.

Table 4-1 presents an equation that expresses the amount of time that you should be in a time-wasting mode when your team is scored upon first, as opposed to a hurry-up mode:

Table 4-1. Statistical determination of when a hurry-up mode of clock management is inappropriate

41.6%	(percentage of times that a blowout occurs by the team who scores first, in other words, the team being blown out should be in a slowdown/time-wasting mode to keep the game as close as possible)
$\pm$ 17.1-19.5%	(percentage of times that a team is scored upon first, but comes back to win; this means that the team that was scored upon first will eventually want to be in a slowdown/time-wasting mode)
58.7-61.1%	(total percentage of instances where it is wrong to go into a hurry-up when you are scored upon first)

The statistics included in Table 4-1 show that well over half the time, if you had chosen to be in a hurry-up mode, rather than a slowdown mode, you would have been in the wrong mode of operation.

In fact, it stands to reason that, since hardly any coaches employ an all-game, clock management strategy, most games have fewer plays and possessions than they would have had if they had been using a strategy of hurrying-up from the moment that their team fell behind. The reason that there are fewer plays is because most teams run their offenses closer to a slowdown mode, rather than a hurry-up mode. This factor also means that a coach who employs a hurry-up mode would many times actually be putting his team in a worse position by hurrying when his team is behind early on, because he would sometimes (41% of the time) be a blowout underdog. By hurrying and increasing the number of possessions, he would be accentuating his own team's relative weakness.

A coach who adopts an inappropriate strategy of increasing the number of plays and presumably possessions would not only be increasing the number of scoring opportunities for his team, but more importantly, he would also be increasing the number of scoring opportunities for his opponent—a team that is superior. Accordingly, assuming that your scoring frequency and your opponent's are always the same, respectively, and that as the blowout underdog, your scoring frequency will be significantly lower than your opponent's, you should be striving for as few possessions as possible for most of the game.

When you are the blowout underdog, you need to keep the game as close as possible, by limiting the number of possessions that both you and your opponent will have. By "flipping the weighted coin" a fewer number of times, you will increase the likelihood of being within striking distance when the game reaches its waning moments. By the same token, at an appropriate point near the end of the game, you *will* eventually have to change the tempo to a hurry-up, in order to make "a push" to win it. "The push" phase will be a topic that will be addressed later in this book.

We employed the tactic of an all-game slowdown a number of times throughout the 1999 season, the first year I took over at Muskego. One such occasion came against a conference rival who was very strong and ranked #1 in the state. They had several Division I-caliber players on a team that had very few, if any, players go both ways. We, on the other hand, were only 2-6, had five sophomores starting, had many two-way players and were definitely blowout underdogs. Our team was in an all-game slowdown, in order to reduce the number of possessions to a minimum—a strategy that almost worked. With only 47 seconds left in the game, we were actually ahead 10-6. To be fair, they had a key injury to their quarterback, which hampered their running attack, but they were still significantly bigger and better. We ended up giving up a long pass to the five-yard line, followed by a quick touchdown, that left the score at 13-10. On our next possession, we threw an interception that was returned for a touchdown, making the final score 20-10.

The key point to keep in mind in the aforementioned case study of how clock management can affect a game is that we came one possession away from pulling off the fluke victory, because we had managed to reduce the number of possessions to nine apiece. On the other hand, if there had been 14 possessions in the game, for example, it would be reasonable to conclude that they would have beaten us by significantly more than 10 points. The fact that *we were* able to shorten the game, in effect, allowed us to be close enough at the end of the game to almost pull off a victory that we would certainly never have had a chance of achieving if we had allowed the game to proceed at any other pace.

Another example of this factor at work occurred in Super Bowl XXXVI, when the New England Patriots were playing the St. Louis Rams. The Rams were 14-point favorites going into the game, one of the largest point-spreads in Super Bowl history. Many pundits had touted the Rams' offense as, perhaps, the best in the history of the NFL and capable of racking up many points per game in a hurry. The players and the media had tabbed the team as "The Greatest Show on Turf."

In my opinion, it appeared that the Pats were trying to take a lot of time off the clock and shorten the game. Well into the third quarter, the New England QB, Tom Brady, had only thrown 16 passes for 86 yards, and the running backs for the Patriots were getting many carries. Brady's final stats were 16 of 27 for 145 yards, 53 yards of which came on the game's final drive while the Pats were in a no-huddle, hurry-up—hardly a windfall of yardage. New England was obviously interested in ball control and time of possession.

The pace of the game was decidedly slow and definitely favored the Patriots, because it kept the number of possessions to a minimum. In fact, the Fox Network did an in-game poll of fans asking which team was gaining an advantage because of the game's pace. Even the public knew, overwhelmingly, that this pace favored the Patriots. The Patriots were regularly running the play clock down into the single digits, although never down to one second, as they probably should have done. At the same time, the Rams did not appear to be trying to conserve the clock or quicken the pace. All of these factors, combined with some very good defensive plays that produced an interception for a touchdown and stifled the Ram offense, allowed the Patriots to be close enough to pull off the "fluke" victory by kicking a 48-yard field goal with no time remaining to win the game 20-17.

The term "fluke" only refers to the pre-game classification of whether or not the Patriots should have been able to win the game, and is in no way meant as a slight to the Patriot coaches or the team. They had a terrific game plan, that put them in the best position to be able to win the game, and the players executed it wonderfully. Patriot's head coach Bill Belichik's post-game conference confirmed the fact that their strategy was based on this premise that they were underdogs. Even though they won the game, he still asserted, "If we're playing next week, we're probably (still) the underdogs, but that's o.k."

Conversely, Mike Martz, head coach of the St. Louis Rams, came out almost one month after the Super Bowl and admitted that the slow pace had hurt his team. He said, "I kind of wish we would have gone to our two-minute offense to start the game." He went on to say, "I was that far from doing it…I wish now that I'd done it, because when we went into the two-minute offense, they couldn't deal with it. When we did it in the fourth quarter, they wore down so quickly." In fact, the Rams did close a 14-point gap late in the game. Imagine what results an all-game hurry-up would have wrought.

The press balked at Martz's comments as Martz had been roundly criticized for not getting the Rams' star running back, Marshall Faulk, enough carries. The press inaccurately assumed that Martz's regret that he hadn't run a hurry-up reflected the fact that he wanted to pass more, since many of Martz's detractors had said that the Rams should have been more "conservative" and given Faulk more hand-offs.

This interpretation is false on two accounts. The first falsehood assumes that by hurrying-up, you must pass the ball. Nothing is further from the truth. The Rams could have run *and* passed more. Both of which would have probably spelled disaster for the Patriots, if the Rams had executed their offense at a rapid pace. The second one assumes that running in a hurry-up means you are being less conservative. Obviously, you can run conservative plays in a no-huddle just as readily as when you *do* in a huddle offense. It seems that Coach Martz was aware of the press' mistaken logic as well. After his initial comments, the press reminded him of other individual's earlier criticism of his "risky" game plan. He responded by saying, "I've never been real concerned about what people think."

☐ If you perceive that your team is not as well-conditioned as your opponent, you should consider wasting time for most of the game. This situation is, of course, not an enviable position. No coach would willingly want to be in this predicament, let alone admit this factor to himself before the game. However, your ability to candidly admit this to yourself may give you an advantage in preparing the most successful clock-management strategy for your team. As a coach, the condition of your squad is one of the few things over which you have control. However, this factor may not be the case or it may be early in the season or any combination of reasons. Whatever the reason, being able to assess your team's lack of conditioning relative to your opponent's can be of useful insight.

If you perceive that your opponent is in better condition than your team, it would behoove you to slow down the tempo, effectively neutralizing a fast pace. Football, as played by most teams, is more anaerobic than aerobic. It is based on expending short bursts of energy, with a good deal of rest in between the bursts. Most plays take the official about 12-15 seconds to set the chains, mark the proper yardage, etc. When added to the 25-second play clock, the resulting scenario involves about 40 seconds of rest, between six- to 10-second bursts. (In the NFL, 40 seconds is the automatic amount of time a team is allotted between most plays, because the NFL's rules committee opted to take out the human error in the referees' ball placing time.) If a team chose to speed the tempo up and snap the ball immediately after the ball was whistled ready for play, the players would only get about 1/3 of the rest time or 12-15 seconds. The point to keep in mind is that if your team isn't as well conditioned as your opponent, take as much time off the play clock as possible to allow them more recovery time.

☐ If you have a significantly greater number of players playing two ways than your opponent, you should consider a slow-paced, time-wasting mode. Somewhat related to the previous scenario, the degree to which your team employs platooning may impact on your clock-management strategy. This factor is, obviously, less critical in college and the pros where players only go one way; however, even at those levels, specialization has become more and more of a factor. Players are constantly coming on and off the field as first-down, third-down, pass-rush, etc. specialists, and are utilized to such an extent that the number of snaps your players get relative to their counterparts can and should become a factor as you decide what tempo your team should operate in.

In this regard, I once made an error in clock management that may have cost my team the game. In 2001, our team was playing a round III quarterfinals game in the WIAA division I playoffs. Because I believed our teams to be fairly evenly matched (we were a slight underdog in our estimation and had lost an earlier meeting with them 13-8), we opened the game in no mode of clock management and waited to see how the game evolved. Although we certainly were not in our fastest mode of operation, the pace proved to be too much for our team and was part of our undoing. The pace we were in was not the *most* conducive pace for success.

On our first possession, we marched 65 yards in 18 plays and scored to go ahead 7-0. It was early November, and the temperature was about 65 degrees, unseasonably warm for Wisconsin, and significantly warmer than it had been in the preceding days and weeks. Our players, as well as theirs, were not ready for the heat—so, the advantage in terms of the heat was a wash. However, the most significant difference was the number of players, linemen in particular, who only went one way for our opponent.

As we came off the field, our linemen looked tired—happy, but tired. I am sure their linemen were tired too. The difference was that when the drive was over, their linemen had a cool, comfortable spot on the bench, with a nice refreshing drink, while our linemen waited briefly for the kick-off team to make the tackle before promptly heading back onto the field. The battle in the trenches never seemed the same the rest of the day, as we struggled with our ground attack.

Exacerbating the problem, we ended up going into our second fastest hurry-up, never recovered, and ended up losing 28-13 to the eventual state runner-up. Perhaps, they would have beaten us anyhow; they were, after all, state runners-up and very well coached. In retrospect, I know that I could have put our players in a much better position to succeed if we had considered this factor and had been in a slowdown from the beginning of the game.

It is interesting to note that when we played this team earlier in the season, we opened up the game in a slowdown due to a missing player, we thought would have a significant impact on our chances of winning the game. The final score of that game ended up at 13-8, with the opponents scoring on their last possession. This example lends support to the coin-flip analogy, which expresses the fact that more possessions will serve to accentuate, the differences between the two teams. Because they had a deeper team, the difference in the second game was accentuated and we lost 28-13—compared to previous game's score of 13-8. In hindsight, we should have been in a much more aggressive slowdown in the second game from the very outset of the game.

As an aside to the aforementioned example, those circumstances reinforce how valuable it is to platoon, if at all possible, in high school. Sometimes, it may not be possible, because of the numbers on your squad or the severe drop-off in ability level after your starters. If it is possible, it can go a long way in diminishing the advantages a team has when it has just a few "studs" who go both ways, instead of a number of more average players who can be spread out over the team and who need to be used only one way.

❑ **When your team is less acclimated to the weather than your opponent, you may consider taking time off the clock.** This factor is something that rarely impacts on a high school game, because opposing teams are generally from a similar, if not identical, geographical location. In college and the pros, however, this factor cannot be overlooked. It can be a key ingredient in the outcome of the game. If it were not potentially a significant element, then the media would not place such an emphasis on it. There would not be nationally televised pre-game shows where the focus of one of the segments is the weather in each NFL game that day. There would not be so many statistics validating the fact that weather can be a prime determiner in the outcome of the game. A stat familiar to most Green Bay Packer and Tampa Bay Buccaneer fans shows that the Bucs have never won a game when the temperature was below 34 degrees.

Almost every coach tries to get his players to understand that the heat, rain, snow, etc., are all extraneous elements and that these factors will not impede his respective team from success. I agree with this approach. It is important to instill in your players a sense of focus on the task at hand, not the weather. But, if you, as a coach, fail to game plan for reality, you could be setting your team up for failure.

Just because you decide that because of the weather, you are going to open up the game with a more deliberate pace does not mean that you have to emphasize this approach to the team. You still emphasize execution, just as you emphasize the need for your players to execute any given play, as opposed to explaining to the team your mid-game philosophy about why you now think a particular formation presents a match-up problem for your opponent. You may not have the time or the inclination to explain this situation to the players, but *you* know why you need to do it; they just need to go out and execute it.

By not turning the game into a marathon session for your players, who are not acclimated to the extremes—particularly the heat, you have leveled the playing field to some degree. Allowing your players to play a shorter game may enable you to keep whatever advantage you have, if you are a pre-game favorite, or stay close before fatigue obliterates your chances of staying close, if you are the underdog.

❑ **When you are planning on your current drive being the last drive of the half by either team, you should waste any extra time, so that your opponent won't be able to use any remaining time to score.** This factor also applies to when you are planning on having your current drive end in a game-winning score. (Many coaches commonly refer to this as "the four-minute drill.") This seems like common sense, but this rule is regularly violated. The idea is to not leave extra time on the clock, which would afford your opponent the opportunity to score. The argument most coaches give in defending their disregard for the amount of time left when they score is, "We'll take the score when we can get it." There is some truth to the fact that you can't necessarily guarantee that'll you'll score with :00 on the clock. On the other hand, blatant disregard for the amount of time left on the clock can and eventually will come back to bite you. Minimizing the amount of time left on the clock before the half ends is too easy to do to disregard this factor.

In a playoff game at the end of the 2001 season, team "A" led team "B" in a low scoring 17-14 game, with less than seven minutes remaining. Team "A" had several opportunities to keep the ball in-bounds at the end of a number of plays (a commonly recognized form of killing the clock). The game was marred by a questionable official's call near the end of the game, allowing team "B" to kick a long field goal with :27 left on the clock, putting the game into overtime. Team "B" consequently went on to win the game. After the game, everyone complained that the referees did a horrible job and that the rule in question needed to be changed. There were dozens of interviews and commentaries from so-called experts who claimed that team "A" was "jobbed" by the officials.

Not one time during the game or afterwards did one of these self-proclaimed experts mention what a horrible job team "A" did in managing the clock. What would it have taken for team "A" to have killed 27 more seconds of the clock in the last few minutes?

In reality, if just one of the times that the running back carelessly ran out of bounds, he, instead, would have stayed in-bounds, team "B" would never have had enough time to kick that field goal. It may also have been possible for the offensive coordinator to call an equally effective running play in lieu of one of the several passing plays that were incomplete and had stopped the clock. Just one in-bounds run, instead of an incomplete pass, would have also killed the clock. A good running play as an alternative to a passing one may or may not have been a viable option. Perhaps there were not running plays available that the coaches felt would have moved the clock and gained more first downs.

While team A's coaches are certainly more familiar with their players and their offensive playbook than anyone else, it is disheartening, though, that some of these drives were not only short in number, but also took little time off the clock and gave the ball back to the opponents on top of it with sufficient time left on the clock. It does not require a stretch of the imagination to conclude that there probably were running plays in team A's playbook that could have gained 0 yards, as did the incomplete pass, and still had the advantage of keeping the clock moving.

Every second you leave on the clock leaves more time for your opponent to run a play. If you are playing for a game-winning or game-tying *field goal*, it is much easier to plan for the half to end with no time on the clock. Once you are in field-goal range, this plan can be as simple as allowing the clock to run down to no more than three seconds before kicking it or calling time out. We script these scenarios in practice so that we have practice calling the timeout at the proper time. We also practice running our field-goal team onto the field and kicking it with three seconds or less on the clock. We have also managed to get our kicks off in as little as nine seconds from the ball being blown dead from the previous play to the time it is kicked.

A situation where the offense is coming off the field and the kicking team is coming on the field should be a carefully choreographed movement. On our team, we take specific steps to ensure that this situation is handled properly. To begin with, we have an area of the team box that we designate as "the bullpen." Encompassing the last five yards of the team box on the sideline on both ends of the field, this area is marked off with large, bright orange traffic cones. No one is allowed to go into the bullpen except for the special teams coaches. They are in charge of calling the various teams to the bullpen, based upon our current field position, down-and-distance, scoring needs, etc. It is not unusual for the bullpen call to change two or three times throughout the course of one drive.

From there, a scenario is scripted, whereby the offense runs a play with around 25 seconds left on the clock, the play is blown dead, and the offense and field-goal teams exchange places. Executing this scenario involves having the bullpen/field-goal team members line up on the 25-yard line, in the exact order that they will be lined up in on the field—the end first, then the tackle, then the guard, etc.. The wings will be lined up on the 26-yard line in order to stay out of the way of the linemen. The kicker and holder will line up on the 27-28 yard line. This group of players will arrive to the spot of the ball from the 50-yard-line-side of the ball, while the offense will exit the field toward the bench from the goal-line side of the ball.

The aforementioned choreography lessens the chance that a collision or delay will occur with our own players. It also lessens the likelihood that we will have some kind of substitution error, because as the players come onto the sidelines, they are reporting directly to the bullpen, where the special teams coaches can count them and verify that we have the proper personnel on the field (this counting method is used with the bullpen for all of our special teams). Obviously, a number of players will not leave the field, because they will be on both the offense and the field-goal team, which makes the transition even smoother. Diagram 4-1 illustrates the transitioning of players on a field-goal attempt toward each end zone.

☐ **When you have the lead and reducing your opponent's "push" time is more important than creating more possessions for your team to score, you should be wasting time.** This factor will be covered in much greater detail in chapter 9, titled "the push." The idea of the push is most closely related to the period in basketball near the end of the game, when the trailing team feels it necessary to go into a full-speed, hurry-up period. This scenario is usually identified by quick shots by the trailing team and very quick fouls on the winning team, in an effort to reduce the time of possession and score quickly.

Diagram 4-1. Transitioning players on a field-goal attempt

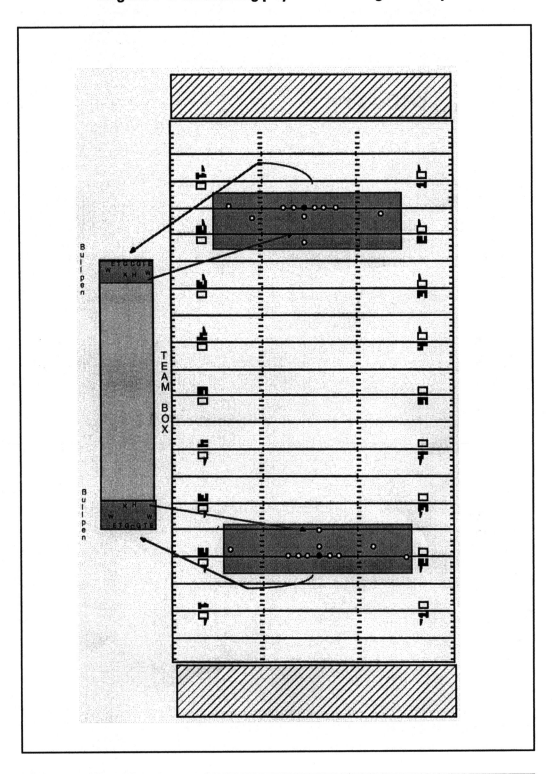

At some point in the football game, the trailing team will probably need to make an all-out effort to make up the difference in the game by increasing the tempo and limiting the opponent's time of possession. The winning team, at this point (a circumstance that will be defined in more detail in "the push" chapter), should increase its time of possession and keep the clock running. This objective is particularly true of a winning team who has been in some form of rapid-paced offense throughout most of the game. At this point, time of possession is more crucial than creating more possessions and/or attempting to score more points.

The idea of not scoring when you have the chance to is a foreign one to most coaches, primarily because they think short-term. "How can more points be a bad thing," they say to themselves. The answer to that is, "when the risk you take by scoring is greater than the advantage you'll gain in scoring those points." We have a number of scenarios where we actually practice *not scoring*. Practicing this scenario is done to help the players understand and not be shocked when the offense is asked not to score in the game. At that point in time, we feel as though scoring, or attempting to score, could put our team in a scenario where we are more likely to lose than the current one we're in.

For example, in one particular game, where we had a one-point advantage with less than a minute remaining and the ball in the red zone, the ballcarriers were told to not score if they had the chance and instead slide down at the 1-yard line. The situation never came to fruition, but at that point in time, the only way the opponent could win was by having us score.

Forcing your opponents to take a lot of time when they have the ball is also critical. It is important to use the clock to your advantage on defense and special teams, not just offense (ways to accomplish this will discussed in a later chapter). The objective in this situation is to end the game as quickly as possible in order to reduce the opponents "push" time, and the possibility that they will make a run at a fluke victory.

☐ **When you want to reduce the number of plays your team must run into an unfavorable wind, you should be wasting time.** This factor is particularly true if your offense is predicated upon the pass. By slowing the pace down and taking as much time off the clock as possible, you will be reducing the amount of time your team must face an unfavorable wind. Wasting time would also be the recommended prescription for your team if it were going to be faced with the prospect of punting or field-goal kicking into a strong wind near the end of the first or third quarter. It may be possible to take enough time off the clock to put the game into the next quarter. This scenario would be an especially enticing prospect, if your opponent has foolishly wasted all of its timeouts.

On one particular occasion when I thought that the wind was such a factor, I committed the so-called "cardinal sin" of coin-flip decisions. On an evening with 50-m.p.h. winds, I instructed our captains to choose to defend an end zone if the opponent won the toss and elected to defer. This scenario was exactly what happened, and we chose to kick-off with a hurricane wind at our backs.

Conventional wisdom says that you always choose to take the ball or defer, because your opponent will get the ball at the beginning of both halves. In this instance, however, I was counting on a number of factors that I considered more important: 1) The field position of our opponent was assuredly going to be poor for the first and third quarter. 2) Because I assessed our teams as being evenly matched, I believed the momentum created by a fast start would be enough to catapult us into a lead that our opponents would not be able to overcome. 3) I did not think either of our offenses was particularly effective, and the huge advantage gained by field position would be the deciding factor. As it turned out, we narrowly won a 7-6 contest. It is a big risk to take, so be sure that it is worth it.

❏ **When your team is beset by sudden injury, sickness, or suspension, you may want to shorten the game by wasting time.** Much of when you should slow down or speed up in these situations will be dictated by when these injuries, etc., occur. On one such occasion, we decided to suspend a dominant offensive lineman, (an individual who had earned all-state honors as a junior) for violating team conduct rules. It had been determined that his suspension would be for one quarter. To diminish the value of his loss to the team, we elected, first of all, to defer. We knew that this would, of course, prompt our opponent to receive (there were no gale force winds that day).

By slowing the tempo on *BOTH* sides of the ball, we were able to have this particular lineman miss a minimal number of plays, seven to be exact. We didn't tell him or the team what we were doing in this regard, because we did not want to appear to be lightening the penalty. In effect, we were able to impress upon the young man being suspended the importance of following the rules, while simultaneously diminishing the negative impact of his loss to his teammates.

Any time you lose a player whose impact on the game you believe will significantly decrease your chances for success, you should consider shortening the game by taking more time off the clock. You are actually following the same logic that you always use to determine the best pace to use, based upon whether or not you believe your team is the favorite or underdog. In the instance where we lost our guard, we thought it took our team from being a slight underdog to being a regular underdog. You may lose players that you believe will not have a significant impact upon who is the favorite. Again, one of your responsibilities as a coach and as someone who is knowledgeable about the team is to be able to assess such a situation and apply the proper clock-management strategy.

The reasons may vary from situation to situation, but the bottom line is, whenever you lose a player, whether it is because of injury, sickness, or suspension, it will usually have some type of impact on the outcome of the game. You should have a contingency plan in mind for the players whom you think would have just such an effect on the game. Planning for and even practicing for such events could give your players and staff confidence that at the least, your team has a plan to go to when the situation does arise.

❏ **When you want to take your opponent out of a fast-paced offense, particularly a passing one, you might want to waste time.** A number of fast-paced offenses exist. Most of these appear to be passing offenses, particularly those that focus on the importance of getting into a rhythm. While some wishbone offenses operate like this, most offenses that focus on rhythm are overwhelmingly pass-oriented. If such a big part of their offense is based on rhythm, tempo, and getting into a groove, it might be worthwhile to consider taking time off the clock to hinder your opponent in that regard.

We have done this on a number of occasions. For example, one such time occurred in 1999, when we were playing a highly regarded passing team in our conference. Their quarterback was rated as high as the #3 recruit in the country at his position (after that season, he earned a scholarship to Northwestern). It was not unusual for that team to throw the ball over 50 times per game. By holding on to the ball for long periods of time, we felt that we were able to take away some of his rhythm and timing. Not only were we taking a lot of time off the clock, but we were also taking a lot of real time as well. Their offense was forced to sit and watch for long periods of real time as well as clock time. Time-of-possession stats were not calculated for that game, but we did have three drives longer than seven minutes and won the game 21-6.

Some of our success in that instance could, undoubtedly, be credited to the frustration the quarterback was feeling. Because his drives were so short and ours were so long, he began to press too hard and make poor decisions. Even when his team was down only 14-0, a deficit that would not necessarily have taken them much time to surmount, he seemed to panic and threw three interceptions. Without question, at least some of his emotional instability was due, in part, to the pace of the game. The game was not fast-paced; it was slow and deliberate. Their short offensive drives, coupled with our long ones, created frustration. Ultimately, they were out of sync (the importance of having a symbiotic offense and defense will be discussed in a later chapter).

On another occasion, when time-of-possession stats were available, and we were employing the same strategy, we held the ball for 19 of the 24 minutes in the second half. Consequently, after having started off the game with a 14-0 deficit, we were able to come back to win the game 35-14. The opponent's offense was most certainly thrown off its rhythm by our offense, which took a lot of time off the clock

❏ **When you want to take an opposing crowd out of a game, one effective way of doing so may involve slowing down the pace and wasting time.** This factor is fairly self-explanatory and, again, perhaps seen more often in the game of basketball. A long, well-sustained, methodical drive may be just the thing to take the excitement out of the game for the home team, whose crowd can fuel enthusiasm for their players.

❑ **When you are close to the end of the first half and wish to make your opponent believe that you are going to try and score even though you are actually content to run out the clock, you are actually trying to waste time by appearing to want to save time.** This technique "does the trick" when you are not yet into the take-a-knee period, because of the combination of the amount of time left on the clock and the number of timeouts your opponent has left (refer to the take-a-knee chart in chapter 8). You may actually trick your opponent into wasting more time for you, because they may not immediately call a timeout.

By running a play, as opposed to taking a knee, you will for a moment *at least,* and maybe longer, cause your opponent to think more about the "x" and "o" strategy than the clock strategy. If you run this play and then quickly race back to the line, even though your intention is to still take up most of the play clock, this step can be even more effective. This scenario could give you just enough time to safely get into the take-a-knee period. Once you have decided that you are not going to attempt to score and are into the take-a-knee period, don't make the mistake of running non-take-a-knee plays, even if they are "just running plays." Such plays involve unnecessary risks. A more in-depth discussion of taking a knee is presented in chapter 8.

❑ **If your defense is more of a "bend-but-don't-break" defense, as opposed to a "big-play" defense, you should consider killing the clock and running at a slower pace.** Your offense and defense will be most effective if they work off the same pace philosophy. This factor is discussed in greater detail in chapter 10, entitled "the Symbiosis of Offense and Defense".

Summary Points

It is important to weigh the value of any of the aforementioned criteria against any other evidence you have in the game that is leading you to believe you should waste or conserve time. Some of the aforementioned items share considerable overlap with one another, and when combined with one or more other items on the list, could be persuasive reasons for you to consider taking time off the clock. As has been mentioned numerous times already, the most important part of this decision is that it requires your opinion as the expert on the game you are playing. It requires careful measurement, insight, and consideration of all the facts and perceptions set out before you. It requires you to do the little things that might give your team the extra edge needed to win the game. It requires you to be a coach!

CHAPTER 5

Reasons to Hurry-Up or Conserve the Clock

Many of the reasons to conserve the clock are the other side of the reasons-to-kill-the-clock coin, so I will be somewhat briefer when reviewing those instances where this is true. Referring back to those items in chapter 4 can help provide you with the rationale necessary to make the proper choice concerning whether to conserve or kill the clock.

❏ **When going into a game and you perceive your team to be a blowout favorite, you should be conserving time for most of the game.** Refer to Chapter 4, which explains why you should waste time when you are a blowout underdog, in order to obtain a much more in-depth discussion of this scenario. You need only to flip-flop the rationale presented in that section to understand this one. Realizing that you are a blowout favorite, you should be doing whatever you can to prevent a "fluke" victory by the blowout underdog. If you and your opponent have more opportunities/possessions, the better team should become more apparent with more possessions. The differences between the two teams will be exacerbated by a greater number of possessions; therefore, when you are the blowout favorite, conserve the clock in order to run as many plays as you can before the "push" period (refer to chapter 9, "the Push," for a more in-depth explanation of this factor).

A good example of how this principle is helpful happened to us on multiple occasions during the 2000 and 2001 seasons. Throughout much of those two seasons, we were classified as blowout favorites. On one such occasion, we were playing at team whose record was 2-6 and was struggling mightily to just finish the season. Later reports from a number of colleagues on that staff told of the low morale and dissension that often accompany such seasons. Although we were much stronger, the game did not start like we had hoped. Miscues and other abnormalities that hadn't previously been a part of our team's repertoire were unexpectedly popping up throughout much of the first half. Surprisingly, we, went into halftime tied at 14-14.

In reality, if we had not been in a hurry-up in the second half, our opponents would have been in a prime position to set themselves up for a fluke victory. Our rapid pace allowed us to score 23 points in the third quarter and go on to win the game, 44-14. If we had been in the clock-killing mode, a pace that most teams unknowingly operate near and one that some coaches advocate, the score would most assuredly have been closer near the end of the game. Who knows what kind of disaster that scenario might have wrought?

Counterpoint Reasons for Conserving Time

The following points are outlined in greater detail in the previous chapter, but from the opposite perspective. By reviewing those counterpoints, you can apply the inverse logic to better understand the next nine factors:

- If you perceive that your team is in better condition than your opponent, you should consider a fast-paced, time-conserving mode for time for most of the game.

- If your opponent has a significantly greater number of players playing two ways than your team, you should consider a fast-paced, time-conserving mode for time for most of the game.

- When your team is more acclimated to the weather than your opponent, you should consider conserving time and running at a fast pace.

☐ **When your opponent appears to be running off extra time before the end of a half in attempt to make their score the last one and leave you no extra time on the clock, you should conserve time so that your team will be able to have enough time to score.** This factor can be a tricky business, because of at least two unknowns: first, you don't know if your opponent is going to score in time; and second, the time you are trying to conserve now could be the time you will be trying to waste if they don't score. This situation will occur because you would be ahead and needing to waste time. This situation would only be the case for end-of-the-game scenarios, as opposed to end of the first half.

❏ **When your team is behind as the blowout underdog at the end of the game, which means you should have been wasting time up to this point in the game, you will more than likely need to go into a hurry-up at some point in the game.** This period is referred to as "the push," and will be discussed in more detail later in the book.

❏ **When you want to increase the number of plays your team must run with a favorable wind at your back, and consequently the number of plays your opponent must run into an unfavorable wind, you should be conserving time.**

❏ **When your opponent's team is beset by sudden injury, sickness, or suspension, presumably making you a blowout favorite, you should be pushing the pace in order to run more plays and accentuate the difference between the teams.** Another reason to consider pushing the pace in this situation involves the fact that your opponent may be forced into playing a number of players who have seen limited action and, as a result, may be rusty, nervous, etc. A no-huddle in this instance would not only take advantage of the inexperienced players, but be unnerving as well.

❏ **When you feel as though a fast-paced rhythm is most conducive to the type of offense that your team runs, as is the case with some passing offenses, you should consider conserving time.**

❏ **When you feel that a fast-pace, coupled with your team's success, could be beneficial in getting your crowd excited and into the game, you should consider conserving time and speeding up the pace.** Although I am not all that crazy about this reason for conserving time, the emotion of the crowd can have a positive impact on the psychological state of many players.

More Reasons for Conserving the Clock

The following reasons to conserve the clock or conserve time are not, as were the points in the previous section, as inversely related to killing the clock. Accordingly, they will be discussed in greater detail than the preceding points in this chapter:

Running in a hurry-up may prevent defensive substitutions. When you are running a no-huddle, which isn't necessarily a hurry-up—because you can still elect to take as much time off the play clock as you wish, you may force your opponent's coaches to keep the same personnel on the field. Many coaches take this approach, because they don't want to risk having the other team snap the ball before they get all of their substitutions into the game. They also realize that rapidly sending players in and out of the game in such instances may cause confusion or lead to a helter-skelter style of play. Instead, they decide to "play it safe and smart" and keep "vanilla" personnel in the game. This can be of great value to you in the game-planning stages, because you are more sure of what type of "look" a defense is going to employ during the game.

This situation is probably more true of the NFL and NCAA, where everybody seems to have some type of pass rush, third down, blitz, or whatever-type of specialist these days. In high school and junior high, this factor is probably less the case and may not be as valid.

A hurry-up may force defensive coordinators into blander play calling. This factor overlaps with some of the principles applicable to the previous point, because some defensive calls will presumably be eliminated from your opponent's play sheet, since the defense may not have the proper personnel on the field for the coach to call a particular defense and no time may exist to get them on. It may also force some defensive coordinators to make more vanilla calls, because it would take too long to call some of the plays that they normally use. Although this reason may cause a team to simplify their play-calling terminology somewhat, it is probably still a deterrent to a number of calls that could be made. More likely than not, this scenario is probably a situation where both the coach and players feel rushed. As a result, in order to instill a sense of calm, the coach reverts back to a "base type" of defense. This reaction is an instinct for many coaches when they feel panicked. This tactic might be particularly useful, if you happen to throw in a hurry-up mode, as a change of pace from a more deliberate pace.

◻ **Being in a hurry-up may incite panic in your opponent.** Similar to other reasons, this factor overlaps with the previous point. In reality, creating chaos on your opponent's team can be very beneficial. The benefits of the enemy panicking are too numerous to mention, but most certainly would include a loss of confidence in themselves and their coaching staff, and a feeling of being unprepared.

The element of surprise has been long regaled in the history of military annals. Many coaches buy into the idea that there are insights to be gained by better understanding circumstances from a military perspective, and this factor is but one of them. One of the biggest keys to Pearl Harbor for the Japanese was the fact that the American forces did not know of the impending attack until the Japanese were upon them—by that time, it was too late.

◻ **A fast-paced offense is more popular.** Although I am generally not in favor of doing anything just because it's popular, but since a lot of people are, it is included in this list of reasons. Creating excitement in your program may be a high priority in reviving it or creating fan interest, which can include alumni with deep pockets. This factor is one of the realities of the world in which we live.

◻ **A fast-pace offense may be more attractive to recruits.** Somewhat related to the sentiments attendant to the previous reason (but a fact nonetheless), it is easier to get kids excited about a fast-paced offense than it is a slowdown. At the college-level, for example, it could be the shot in the arm that puts a recruiting program "over the edge" compared to its rivals.

❏ **A no-huddle, rapid-pace offense may cause your opponent to call a timeout.** One reason for this type of timeout is related to the fact that a coach might need to use a timeout to settle his troops down. A coach who is not expecting such a tactic might need it to confer with his coaches and players to decide how best to proceed for the rest of the game. If this situation appears to be the case, you should come out of the timeout in your previous (more-conventional) huddling mode. Subsequently, when you decide to go back to the no-huddle later in the game, the opponent's players and coaches may have forgotten some of the strategy in defending your team in this mode of attack and be caught off guard. This situation might even be enough to force your opponent to call another timeout.

Another reason for calling a timeout in this instance may be to allow the players to catch their breath. This factor would, of course, overlap with an earlier point about your team's physical condition relative to your opponent's.

❏ **Changing to a fast pace might jump-start your team or get an opponent out of its groove.** Changing to a fast pace could be used to get momentum rolling your way. "Old Mo", as some coaches say, can be an invaluable ally. Momentum is difficult to get back once it is lost and a fast pace may provide you with a means to do so, when other avenues have failed.

❏ **Being able to use a no-huddle offense in the middle of the game will give your players more confidence and practice for those circumstances when you need to use it in the "two-minute" situation.** We used the no-huddle offense extensively in the middle of our games during the 2001 season. As a result, on those occasions when we needed to execute it, near the end of the half or the end of the game, our players had a much stronger level of confidence in being able to proficiently operate in it.

Using a no-huddle offense in the middle of the game probably spells out the fact that you will have a larger part of your offense available in this mode than other teams who relegate their no-huddle usage to "two-minute" drills exclusively. Many coaches talk about their "two-minute" drill, as if it were some type of secret operation, that has only distant connection to the rest of the offense. They talk of a set number of plays, or even a pattern of the same types of play over and over again. Almost to a coach, each coach will admit that the two-minute part of his team's game plan is a fraction of the rest of the offense.

Because we wanted to be able to run a normal offense in our no-huddle mode, we had to become more efficient with our terminology, so we would not be handcuffing ourselves with a limited play-selection. As a result, we were able to run over 98% of our entire offense out of the no-huddle. Our offense, with no exaggeration, has over 5000 formations that the players were easily able to understand and operate in. We were able to use almost all of the plays that were otherwise at our disposal in a huddling offense, while we were in the no-huddle mode. Over the course of the entire 2001 season, we ran 698 offensive plays and did not have a single formation mistake. The 698 plays that we ran involved well over 300 different formations.

The key point to emphasize in this instance is that reducing terminology and increasing simplicity allowed our offense to operate more efficiently in both the no-huddle and huddling modes of our offense. It enabled us to become much more diverse and flexible in how we chose to attack any given opponent. It allowed us to confuse our opponents without confusing ourselves. Because blocking rules and formation terminology were simplified, it became relatively simple for players to know who to block based upon where they were lined up.

On several occasions, I can recall calling a play from a formation that we had never even practiced before—an act that is supposed to be one of the other "Cardinal Sins" of coaching. However, when the players came out of the huddle, they never looked over to the sidelines and shrugged as if to express confusion, nor did they have the whispering-conversations amongst themselves, like you often see when players are unsure of their responsibilities. Instead, they confidently executed the play that was called. The first time that this happened the play actually went for a 60-yard touchdown—so much for this particular "Cardinal Sin."

❑ **Using an all-game or mid-game no-huddle increases what your opponent will have to prepare for.** This need for extra preparation might occur in a few ways. First, because you are running more plays, the volume of information that the opponent must sift through can increase by as much as one-third. As a result, they have more work to do. Although this factor isn't an overwhelming advantage, it is something. It also means they might need to take *extra* measures in their classroom meetings and on-the-field efforts with the players in order to fully prepare for your team. Another disadvantage that is created for the opponent in this regard is that they will need to teach their scout team how to no-huddle, a monumental task in mere days for a team that does not extensively use it.

❑ **Playing in an all-game no-huddle means that you should practice in an all-game no-huddle, which means that you will get more plays and more repetitions in practice.** Every coach I know talks about the importance of getting reps, but many teams don't get the kind of repetitions they need to become proficient. I have been on staffs where after a play is run, some coach stops the action, and we have a three-minute pow-wow over who was supposed to block whom, and what exactly went wrong during the play. After these issues finally get it cleared up to run the play again, and the next play is actually run, the same scenario plays itself out all over again. By the end of the 25-minute team period, we have run a grand total of eight plays. Most of these plays are only run one time. This situation is ludicrous. It is hard to get good at anything by doing it only once a day.

We encourage our coaches to "coach players on the fly" during this period, offering short bursts of feedback, so that the tempo is not affected. If something needs to be emphasized in more detail, a coach can always bring a player or group of players into our office after practice and review the mistake on film (a good reason to film practices). In the event that there is a nuclear-bomb type mistake, we *will* stop the session and fix the problem before resuming practice. These instances, however, are few and far between.

Because we practice our team offense in a no-huddle mode, we run many more plays. In a 20-minute period, we have run over 40 plays on a number of occasions. When combined with the repetitions from other parts of practice, it is not unheard of for our players to have run over 80 plays in a single practice.

❏ **Practicing in a no-huddle means that you should not have to spend as much time during your conditioning periods.** As you can imagine, running more than 40 plays in a 20-minute time frame can be very fatiguing. In this instance, the no-huddle practice serves a number of purposes. For example, our players aren't practicing "running;" they are practicing football-specific conditioning. Furthermore, because we are saving time that might otherwise be devoted to "pure" conditioning, we have more time to devote to practicing what might need extra attention at that given moment.

As opposed to getting good at running cross-fields, gassers or whatever your favorite conditioning drills are, your players will get good at football. By practicing at a fast-pace, they will have the benefit of their body learning proper neuromuscular, football-specific patterns while in a fatigued state. In other words, they will be practicing how to use the proper football techniques you have taught them in the "individual-drilling" segment of practice while they are tired. Truth be known, that sounds a lot like how we want them to perform on game day. Practicing in this manner will more readily simulate the type of physical duress and pace they will experience during the game, than the type of practice where "Coach Longwind" has to hear himself talk every three minutes.

You shouldn't get the idea that we don't condition, because we do. We run sprints like most teams, but we don't have to devote the amount of time to be in relatively great shape that this endeavor requires solely to the "conditioning" phase of practice. In fact, most of our players tend to run harder during the conditioning session, because it is not an all-day affair. When they get to the "team" portion of practice when we run our offense, they are conditioning again, but they don't perceive it to be conditioning.

❏ **By practicing in a no-huddle mode, your defense will be more prepared for the time that your opponent does it in the game.** This factor is fairly self-explanatory. Your players will become accustomed to how to get calls and to line up quickly and calmly, even if they are simulating another team's defense. For this purpose, we will sometimes have our scout team line up in our own defense, just for practice. It is also not uncommon for an opponent to play some of the same fronts that we do, so this task serves two masters.

❏ **Practicing in a no-huddle keeps the tempo and attention of the players at a more desirable level.** A lot more is going on in a no-huddle practice. There are many more things to pay attention to and more opportunities for the back-ups to see the field. As a result, there is less of the inattentiveness that often accompanies many of the practices, where players get good at amusing themselves and getting on the nerves of the coaches.

❏ **Practicing in a no-huddle means that your practices can be shorter.** Our on-field portion of practice never once went over the two-hour mark during the 2001 season. We make it a priority to be on time for all drills and segments by using a horn, so all parts of the program, freshmen through seniors, must rotate to the next segment. By keeping the amount of time on the field at a reasonable level, the players' attention span is more focused.

Limiting the amount of time that has to be spent on practice also enables us to treat our players with dignity and respect for their lives outside of football. Because players tend to have a variety of outside interests (family, friends, girlfriends, jobs, studies, etc.), when we ask them for two hours of their time it is not an unreasonable request. In turn, we can ask for and expect a high level of commitment to the task at hand, without worrying as much about their minds wandering. All factors considered, it gives our program more validity in the school, the community and the players' homes, because when we ask our players to become better people by being involved in our football program, we also keep the time commitment to do so in proper perspective, while encouraging them to learn about the importance of their commitment to the team.

❏ **At the lower levels of high school and junior high, a no-huddle system will allow for a greater number of players to get playing time.** This factor involves simple math. By running more plays in a game, you will be able to rotate more players into the game. This step will help keep the "coaches" in the stands relatively happy. Getting as many players into the game as possible is one of the few instances where the "fans in the stands" actually have the right perspective about matters related to the game. Football at the youth-league level should be about getting all players who follow the team rules playing time on game day. Every youth coach who is reading this book should consider this factor to be more important than any other point in this or any other instructional book on football.

Summary Points

As you can see, the applications and reasons for the no-huddle/hurry-up mode are many and varied. Ranging from having more game time to conducting a more-efficient practice, this mode has many potential benefits. As with the "clock-killing" mode, they must be weighed against the other priorities within your system. Some of these are ones that you should employ in your program, particularly the ones related to practice organization, while others are more dependent upon in-game scenarios. Just remember that football-life in the fast lane can be one of the most productive tools you have.

CHAPTER 6

How to Operate
a Slowdown Tempo

At Muskego, we call clock management our "dictated tempo" philosophy. We want to determine at what tempo the game is going to proceed. Since nobody has ever attempted to manage the clock for the entire game like we do, we have always had our way in this endeavor and have had a distinct advantage over our opponents because of it. We have six modes of operation: Hammer I, Hammer II, Arrow, Warpath I, Warpath II, and Victory.[1]

One idea that we incorporated into our program was the use of painted signs to indicate the tempo we are in. These signs are old down markers, that I spray-painted. The green sign, our Hammer I and II modes, tells the players we will be in one of our two types of slowdown/clock-killing. The red sign, which represents Warpath I and II, tells our players to be in one of two types of hurry-up. The yellow sign represents an interim pace, while the white sign refers to our take-a-knee mode.

---

1 *Many of the methods and steps used to incorporate these modes of operation into our program have been adopted and modified from other coaches and other sources, including John Reed's* Football Clock Management. *These "ideas" have been modified to meet our unique needs and beliefs, as needed. While differences sometimes exist in the philosophies that coaches have regarding when and why to conserve or kill the clock more often than not, several similarities exist in how they go about operating in those modes. This circumstance is partially because some of the methods used are or should be obvious and universal methods of clock control. Still other methods will presumably be revelations.*

The sign is displayed at all times on the sideline for the players on the field to see. We are sure to call attention to any time the sign changes so that the quarterback or linebackers can alert the rest of the team. Players are then aware that the sign being displayed dictates all of their actions related to that mode of tempo operation.

HAMMER I

Our most often-used slowdown tempo is Hammer I. The following list details how we will operate in Hammer I:

☐ **Offense:**

• **We want to snap the ball with no less than 23 seconds elapsed off the play clock.** We do this by using a human play clock, whereby one of the coaches will wind his arm to indicate the number of seconds left on the clock. Many refs will allow us up to 26 or 27 seconds to snap the ball. They seem to have the attitude that, "If you're close, we'll let it go." Of course, in high school, there is no visible play clock. Instead, most officials have a buzzer on their belt or on their watch that tells them the play has gone 25 seconds. It is only because I have heard the buzzer go off on a number of occasions that I have been able to observe this apparent leniency. In college and the pros, the play clock would, of course, be adhered to much more carefully. On occasion, we will actually try to "scout" some of the refs during the game to get an idea of how much we can get away with by letting the quarterback get gradually closer to the 25-second mark.

• **Stay in bounds as the ballcarrier at all times.** The only exception to this stipulation would be if the ballcarrier feels that he must go out bounds in order to get the first down. This guideline is one of the primary differences between Hammer I and Hammer II. If a situation should arise, for instance, where the ballcarrier is confronted by a defender at the line-to-gain near the sideline, and he must lower his shoulder, but in so doing realizes that his momentum will carry him out of bounds, he should try to get the first down. At this point in the game, maintaining possession and moving the sticks are more important than staying in bounds.

• **Prefer the run over the pass.** In other words, we want to enhance the likelihood that the clock will keep moving. If you throw the ball, you will inevitably throw incompletions and stop the clock. If you feel you must throw the ball in order to move the sticks, than do so. The Patriots ran the ball for the majority of the game in Super Bowl XXXVI, and by doing so, were able to shorten the game and the number of possessions. They were able to "flip the coin" a fewer number of times. It should be noted that while they did still throw the ball, it was done more judiciously than they appeared to do during the rest of their season.

• **Prefer to run outside the hashes.** This factor is a consideration that occasionally comes into our play calling, but is generally left near the bottom of the priority list. The reasoning behind this factor is that running outside the hash will take longer than running up the middle, and it will also force the official to take longer spotting the ball. Most officials appear to take approximately 12-15 seconds to spot the ball. Running outside the hash can extend this time. However, plays that will gain you first downs should be run before you prioritize this factor.

- **Prefer not to call timeouts.** Don't stop the clock unless you really have to. Generally speaking, it is a waste of a potentially valuable resource to ever call a timeout on offense. Timeouts should be saved for defense, when they can save you the most time. On offense, you have more control over how much time you spend anyway, so why not save the timeouts to use for a time when you don't have as much control over how time is spent. This factor is another way that football has advantage over basketball. For the most part, the only reason you should ever call a timeout on offense is at the end of a half if you didn't need to call them for any reason while you were on defense. On the other hand, depending on the circumstances, they should not automatically be "saved for good measure" for the end of the game, in lieu of using them for an *appropriate* reason (e.g., save time) earlier in the game.

In one particularly big game we played, we were winning the game by eight points with around seven minutes left in the game. We had just recovered a fumble around the 50-yard line and were methodically marching down the field in a Hammer II mode (another time-wasting mode that will be explained in greater detail later in this chapter). We ended the drive on the 12-yard line, with a 29-yard field goal to go ahead 50-39 with 1:41 left to play in the game. The opposing coach had opted to not call a timeout during our drive, which ended up costing him over two minutes of clock time. Had he called three timeouts while his team was on defense, he would have lengthened the amount of time his team had to score. If he had spent his timeouts sooner, his final drive would have started with over three and half minutes at least.

Instead, he saved them for offense, where he ended up calling two timeouts on the next drive. Those two timeouts ended up saving him a grand total of about 25 seconds. They ended up scoring with :04 on the clock and missed the two-point conversion to bring the score to 50-45. We recovered the ensuing onside kick, and the game was over. Had they chosen to use the timeouts when they were on defense, they would have given themselves a much more favorable scenario, with our team possibly having to actually run plays at the end of the game, instead of taking-a-knee. They also may have been able to kick it deep and pin us back, giving them the chance for better field position. They probably still would have lost, but the scenario wouldn't have been as bleak. Regardless of the outcome, you can see that they cost themselves over ninety seconds of clock time and virtually eliminated any chance that they might have had to win with the one timeout that they were "saving" presumably for a field-goal attempt. Your job as the coach is to put your team in the best-case win scenario. Saving the timeouts to use on offense put our opponent in a less-likely-to-win scenario.

You should spend the timeouts on defense to allow yourself more time to score, rather than save timeouts for offense for a field goal that you may not even use. You have more chances to stop the clock by your own doing on offense anyhow.

- **If a timeout is required in the Hammer I mode, wait for the play clock to run down to one second before calling it.** We are careful to have the quarterback practice how to do this. He cannot tell the official, "I want a timeout with one second on the play clock," for two reasons. First, we don't want the official to mistakenly call timeout before the clock gets to one second, because he only listened to the first part of the sentence, "I want a timeout..." Second, most officials will make *the player himself* actually call the timeout with one second left; therefore, the player must stand by the official and watch the human play clock on the sideline until it gets to one second *and then* call the timeout. If the official asks him he should either say, "With one second on the play clock, I want a timeout," or wait until the clock gets to one second to call it without forewarning the official.

- **Have your players disguise the pace.** When I was working with high school freshmen team in 1998, we did not do this. We had the team come to the line and get set with the quarterback under center, looking at the coach/human play clock on the sideline. Aside from the fact that it was very unpopular with the fans (even our own), the officials started to sometimes hurry their ball-placing routine, probably because they were making a conscientious effort to be unbiased.

If you disguise your pace, many of the officials will go about their business in their "normal" pace, which is slower. We do this by having the quarterback hold the play calling in the huddle a little longer, and holding the team at the line a bit longer. For example, if the quarterback gets the team to the line too early, he will waste any extra time that may still be on the play clock by stepping back from the center and "checking the formation" and "looking over the defense". Although he may actually be doing these things, he may not be doing them at all, but just be giving the appearance of doing them, so that he can waste time in a more inconspicuous way.

We try to emphasize the aforementioned methods of slowing down the clock, as opposed to having our players walk to the line, which is another method of wasting time. Because walking to the line may have the psychological disadvantage of promoting laziness, we try not to emphasize it. While the players do tend to get the line slower when we disguise the pace, because they are getting more chance to rest, at the same time, we are not promoting a lack of hustle.

- **Leave the ball on the ground after the play.** Don't be a jerk, and throw the ball down like many of the NFL players always seem to do. Instead, leave the ball lying on the ground where you landed. Picking the ball up from the ground and spotting it properly will take the official extra seconds, which add up over the course of the game. If it takes the official even as little as two extra seconds to do this, multiplied by an average number of plays per game (50), that is 100 extra seconds. Some coaches will choose not to emphasize this factor because it is "a minor detail." But, games are often won and lost by minor details!

What would you say to one of your players if he did his curl route at 20 yards, instead of the 17 yards you wanted, and then exclaimed in a coach-like, gruff, condescending voice, "Gimme a break, coach, it's only a couple yards." Undoubtedly, you would find his actions to be unacceptable and would certainly bench this player until he came around to your way of thinking, which involves everyone (players and staff alike) being particular about the details, however small.

Yet, there are many coaches who will dismiss the importance of such small notions, as being a relatively unimportant part of the game, and "a little thing." They think that scheming and diagramming and blocking and tackling are all that wins games. I tell our players that everybody can do the big things. That's called being average. Doing the little things is what separates the champions from the average.

Every coach who is worth his weight will diagram, scheme, and teach blocking and tackling. Some, however, won't pay enough attention to details, like this factor, that can separate themselves from the ordinary. At best, their actions (or lack thereof) are confounding.

How many close games have you had where you thought that, "just one or two little things were the difference in this game"? What would you give to go back and change those little things now? Don't be duped by the bravado demeanor of many coaches who would say that this is an unimportant part of the game. Ours is a society, where football players are allowed to do self-serving, dumb dances after every tackle they make, without so much as a penalty or even a tongue-lashing from their coaches, because these attention-drawing antics are accepted as an "important part of the game." Coaches and players associated with these shenanigans claim that these "little things" help them keep their head in the game. How foolish. If players are allowed to do such little dumb things, you (as the coach) should have the wherewithal to do the "little smart things" that *do actually* make a difference in the outcome of the game.

• **Consider running only quarterback keepers when only one more first down is needed to put your team into the take-a-knee period.** In fact, you should consider running quarterback keepers, period, regardless of how much time is left. We regularly run what most people call "quarterback sneaks" as a part of our middle-of-the-field-offense. It makes the defense continue to have to defend the entire field, in spite of the fact that you may be running a no-back or spread formation. Because we don't just run this play in short-yardage situations, we have considerable success.

Try running the quarterback keeper on first-and-10, second-and-long, or third-and-four, in the middle of the field, when the defense isn't expecting it, and you will often gain at least five yards. It has the added advantage of being a very low-risk play. If you are too worried about getting your quarterback injured, you might consider running the same blocking scheme, but giving the ball to the fullback. Our fullback gained over 900 yards and 5.8 yards/carry on this play alone in 2001. It does, however, have the added risk of involving another exchange and taking slightly longer to develop than a quarterback sneak, which can give the defense slightly more time to react.

• **Don't unpile quickly, but coach sportsmanlike conduct.** On the other hand, your players can take more time off the clock by being deliberate in how they get off the pile. For instance, not helping people off the pile takes longer than if you help them. This step may be only a little detail, but remember that you expect it of your players; they should expect it of you. Constantly coach them on doing the "little" things.

• **In the event that there are only 10 men on the field, consider running the play anyway.** We have coached our quarterback to consider whether or not the player missing is critical to the success of the play, when compared to the benefit of keeping the clock going. It has not come up in a game, but it is a detail that we continue to remind him of in case it does. It could cost us as many 45 seconds later in the game, if we should need to stop the clock when the opposing team is on offense. If we don't have that timeout, that is around 40-45 seconds that we gave the other team to waste, because we did not "contingency" plan. Coaches contingency plan for all kinds of other situations that aren't ideal; why not plan for not having enough players on the field too?

HAMMER II

Hammer II is the same as Hammer I, except for the following factors:

• **The ballcarrier must keep two hands on the ball at all times.** We probably go overboard more than other programs in teaching proper ball carrying, and this is one example. The technique we teach for holding the ball with two hands is discussed in greater detail in chapter 11—"How to Practice Clock Management".

• **Players must stay in bounds.** This factor differs from Hammer I, because it applies even if the player thinks he can gain a first down if he goes out of bounds. At this point in the game, staying in bounds is prioritized over gaining another first down, because keeping the clock moving is an essential. Whether staying in bounds causes the opponent to call a timeout or allows the clock to keep running, you are ultimately coming closer to winning than if you had stopped the clock, gone out of bounds, and gotten the first down.

• **When you are going to run a play that goes from Hammer time to a take-a-knee period, because the runner will gain a first down, have the ballcarrier slide to the ground after gaining the first down.** Doing anything else is an unnecessary risk.

↠ When should your team go into Hammer II?

The point at which you should go into Hammer II is a function of five variables, which may or may not overlap each other with regards to which one you consider is most important at the time: 1) how much of a lead you have; 2) how many timeouts your opponent has; 3) how much time is left in the game; 4) what your field position is; and 5) how successfully your opponent can move the ball. If you are in the shadow of your own goal post with a one-point lead and 2:25 left in the game, and your opponent has three timeouts remaining, and has been easily moving the ball, you *would not* want to go into Hammer II. Your opponent could stop the clock and force a punt, which would give them excellent field position. Because you would want to improve your field position, you would need first downs. In Hammer II, you must stay in bounds and that restriction might prohibit you from being able to get first downs.

However, if your opponent had no timeouts left, and you had the ball on their 20 yard-line with the same time remaining, and they have not been moving the ball successfully, you *would* want to go into Hammer II. Because they can't stop the clock, and it is unlikely that if you run out of downs they will be able to score, your priority should be on keeping the clock running. This situation involves a common-sense function with many different scenarios, and you—as the expert of the game—need to be able to surmise which mode gives your team the best chance for victory.

☐ Defense:

• **Tackle your opponent inbounds and upright.** The clock needs to keep running, so obviously tackling inbounds is a priority. The reason a player should tackle upright is two-fold: 1) The whistle won't blow as quickly when the ballcarrier is upright; and 2) much of the way that tackling and weightlifting are to players is more congruent to tackling upright. Squatting, dead lifting and Olympic lifts do not have anything to do with tackling to the ground. In fact, historically, only a few tackling drills have actually promoted tackling to the ground. It seems that most coaches teach a progression that finishes with both the tackler and the person being tackled both in the upright position.

The aforementioned does not mean a player should be chastised for tackling someone to the ground in the game. After all, getting the player stopped is the tackler's number one priority and sometimes the only way to do so is to take him to the ground. The key point is we don't emphasize it in our drills. It doesn't perpetuate the proper form that should happen on a form tackle. Very few tackles are actually form tackles and, in reality, happen as a result of a player's instinct, reactions, and athletic ability. We will yell at a player if he unnecessarily carries a player out of bounds and stops the clock, however.

- **Prefer to not call timeouts. Any stoppage of the clock will hurt your cause in this mode.** There are enough natural stoppages in the game that don't need to be compounded by you intentionally stopping the clock yourself.

- **If you must call a timeout have a designated player, probably an inside linebacker, call it just before the quarterback gets into position to take the snap.** Don't wait until the quarterback is under center to call a timeout, because he could go on a silent count.

- **Avoid "prevent" defenses until the last play of the game.** Prevent defenses generally allow too much yardage to be gained. The objective is to make your opponent take as much time as possible getting down the field. If you are in a prevent defense, where defensive backs are 20-25 yards downfield, this alignment allows the receivers to not only pick up substantial yardage, but usually get out of bounds as well.

When we are faced with this scenario on defense, we emphasize that we don't want to get beat deep. Having the receivers catch the ball is alright, but keep the man in front of you. In the 2001 season, we were beating a team by 11 points with 1:41 left in the game. They had to score twice in less than two minutes to beat us—a very unlikely scenario. We told the DB's to make sure that the opponents took up as much time as possible getting down the field. This situation was alluded to earlier in the book, where our opponents used two of their three timeouts on the drive, drove 83 yards, scored a touchdown with :04, missed the two-point conversion and died with one "field-goal" timeout in their pocket..

By not playing a prevent defense, we made them take up time to score. Because the score ended up 50-45, I was not as much concerned about them scoring, as I was about when they were going to score. We had both proven that we could easily move the ball on each other, so I was not confident in our ability to *stop them from scoring*. I was counting more on our ability to *slow them from scoring*.

- **Unpile deliberately.** Concerning this factor, refer to the explanation that was discussed earlier in this chapter on the same topic.

❏ Special Teams:

- **Snap the ball with less than five seconds on the play clock.** This factor is different than the offensive tactic of snapping with one or two seconds on the play clock, because the punting and field-goal units, both of which require long snapping, can be timed by the defense. It is more critical to keep the defense off guard, so that they cannot time the snap and block a kick. This stipulation is also different than offense, because the defense cannot be certain where the ball is going, as opposed to the field-goal and punt plays where the destination of the ball is much more probable. Personally, I learned about this factor from my own team's mistakes.

We had never had a punt blocked on any team that I had coached until the 2001 season, when we had three of them blocked. Along with having the wrong personnel on the field, which was my mistake, we realized that the defenses were timing their rushes exceptionally well, because our snap counts were too predictable. By giving our center a five-second window to snap the ball on his own silent count, the defenses had to play us honestly and could not get such a big jump.

• **Consider a deliberate bloop, or an onside kick, or kick out of bounds when your team is ahead by 9-16 points and two minutes or less are left in the game.** The onside kick is the type of kick that is least likely to be returned for a touchdown. On the other hand, you must drill this type of kick with your kick-off team, because an alert returner may catch the ball in an upright position and attempt to run it back (we encourage our players to do this unless we are in a "take-a-knee" period). Bloop kicks, as well, are generally returned by players who are not the best athlete, so kicking to these players has a lower probability of being returned for a touchdown.

In terms of kicking out of bounds, frankly, I am not sure why teams don't do this more often, especially at the lower levels of competition. Possibly, one of the biggest reasons that coaches don't do it is because it is very unpopular. In our situation, the "coaches in the stands" regularly express their disapproval of this tactic. Regardless, we coach our players to understand all of the possible benefits of kicking out of bounds in order to build up their resilience and resolve for those situations when we decide to do so. Furthermore, most high-school kickers can't kick far enough to make kicking the ball deep a worthwhile endeavor.

In fact, when we analyzed our 1999 stats, we found that our opponents' average starting field position after a deep kick was the 31.4-yard line. Because of this, in 2000 and 2001 well over 50% of our kick-offs were kicked deliberately out of bounds. Even when our opponents opted to have us re-kick with the five-yard penalty, that meant that the average field position would be the 36.4-yard-line (a mere 1.4 yard cost to us to find out what our opponent would do), which some coaches refer to as a "good" starting field position. In reality, it could be questioned whether this is really the case (a factor that will be discussed in greater detail later in this section).

The reasoning for our kicking out of bounds was, "Why risk kicking the ball deep for the three extra yards that we would put our opponent back?" Aside from the fact that putting your opponents three yards further back is not a huge distance, it has one definite advantage: a ball kicked out of bounds will never be returned for a touchdown. For us, especially in a league that regularly had a great number of "open-field" athletes, it was not worth it to kick deep. Furthermore, it was not worth it to possibly gain three yards and risk having a touchdown scored against us in the process. It was like playing Russian roulette. Finally, since most coaches opt to take the ball at the 35-yard line, because it is "good" field position, we didn't have to worry about the five-yard penalty and re-kick.

In reality, the 35-yard line is not particularly conducive to scoring. While every coach would prefer to have their opponent start at the 1-yard line, this possibility carries with it certain inherent risks—in particular, kicking the ball down the middle of the field in the attempt to pin the opponent deep carries the risk of a possible long return or touchdown. As such, starting a drive at the 35-yard line does not seem so bad in comparison.

One uncredited study I found, calculated scoring probabilities for drives that had different starting points on the field. According to that study, a drive that started between the –0 and –20-yard lines had a one-in-30 chance of scoring. A drive starting at this field position, as the result of a kick return, does not happen very often. A drive that starts between the –20 and –40 yardline had a one-in-18 chance of resulting in a field goal or a touchdown. Between the –40 and 50-yard line, it was one in five. Accordingly, the risk of kicking the ball down the field for the few times that you will be able to actually pin your opponent deep does not appear to justify the risk of having a big kick return or even a touchdown executed against your team.

In 2000 and 2001, we had offenses that were considerably above average for the Milwaukee area, averaging 306 and 317 yards per game respectively. The most interesting statistic related to this situation, however, was the fact that in both years, the average drive was only approximately 30 yards.

Given that we had an above-average offense, one that averaged only 30 yards per drive, it could be reasonably concluded that the average offenses would average far less than this. Accordingly, if a good offense can move the ball 30 yards from the 35-yard line, that would mean it would end its drive at the opposite 35 yard line, which is typically thought of as a no-man's land—too short to try to punt and too long for a field goal. The opponents, then, end up taking over themselves in so-called "good" field position.

At this point, imagine you have an offense that averages closer to the more typical average of, perhaps, 15-yard drives. You end your drive at the 50, punt for 30 yards to the 20, where we return the ball eight yards (our 2000 and 2001 combined punt-return average) to the 28—only seven yards short of where you began your drive. This ball placement does not seem like the good starting field position every announcer always said it would be. Suddenly, especially when weighed against the risks and benefits of kicking deep, that "good" field position begins to seem rather pedestrian and not such a bad place to have your opponents start their drive on many occasions.

The bottom line in this instance is that kicking the ball out of bounds on the kick-off may be one of the best options you have, regardless of whether or not you are ahead. It does, however, carry with it the disadvantage of not running as much time off the clock, but it might be worth it. It seems to be particularly effective when it is mixed in with bloop and squib kicks. Opposing coaches seem less apt to want to accept the penalty and take the re-kick when this tactic is mixed in with other types of kicks. These coaches think they are "taking advantage of your mistake and misfortune" of having kicked out of bounds and choose instead, to accept the ball on the 35-yard line.

The best situation of all would, of course, be if your kicker is capable of kicking the ball into the end zone, in high school, or past the end line, in the NCAA and NFL, where the kick is a touchback and comes out to the 20. If our kicker has a strong enough leg, or a favorable enough wind to threaten this type of depth, we will allow him to kick deep. It also serves as a change-up kick, so our opponent will tend to take kicks out of bounds at the 35-yard line, instead of penalizing us and making us re-kick as previously discussed. Even if they do make you re-kick once, it is worth the 1.4 yards that you will lose finding this out.

• **Consider letting rolling scrimmage kicks keep rolling.** A scrimmage kick is usually a punt or field goal, but could be a drop kick or quick kick as well. Remind your players that a blocked field-goal attempt is the same as a blocked punt. The decision whether to have a member of the kicking team touch a rolling kick and down it will depend more upon whether you are in Hammer I or Hammer II, than which direction the kick is rolling.

Most coaches will tell their players to let it roll if it is going toward their opponent's goal line and down it if it rolling backward toward their own. Assuming that the ball is not in danger of rolling into one of the end zones the decision to touch it or not should be based more on the mode you are in. In Hammer II, we will let it roll, regardless of the direction it is rolling. In fact, many times we won't even put a return man deep. In Hammer I, we will stop it if it looks like it will roll more than five yards toward our end zone.

• **Consider quick kicking on third-and-long or fourth-and-short.** Of all the strategies that make sense in football, this tactic is the one that most coaches appear to fear most. Although the logic of this tactic is many times sounder than going for the first down, several factors are commonly advanced concerning why this never happens, including: nobody else does it, so it must not be sound; coaches have too much pride and bravado to "waste" an opportunity and intentionally give the ball to the opponent; and it can be wildly unpopular with the fans and to whatever other people the coach tends to listen.

With regard to the first reason, for a group of people who let on to be a rough-and-tumble sort and who (allegedly) forge on courageously and independently in their thinking, coaches are sometimes among the most insecure group one can envision. Many coaches are afraid of the possible repercussions of doing anything that so overwhelmingly contradicts conventional wisdom. For example, many coaches scoffed at the likes of Clark Shaughnessy and Knute Rockne, when they were revolutionizing the passing game. It wasn't until everyone was doing it that it became recognized as a viable means of moving the ball. Coaches are generally afraid to try anything that might appear to be considered maverick.

Concerning the second reason, many coaches are often unable to see past the immediate future and the benefits that an apparently poor, short-term decision will have in good, long-term game planning. Such vision requires a "small bit" of imagination, and a "large look" at the statistics to understand that the benefits of quick kicking outweigh whatever immediate disadvantage that might occur.

When you quick kick the defense is typically not expecting it, or feels compelled to defend a possible offensive play, so they choose to not put a returner deep. Furthermore, when the ball is kicked end over end as it is supposed be when it is quick kicked, it is not unusual for it to roll a considerable distance. As a result, a good quick kick may go in excess of 50 yards on a regular basis if you have a capable person to kick it. Because quick kicks are not returned, the net punt yardage is the same as the punt itself. The fact that there is no return on a dangerous open-field play like the punt return should be reason enough to use it, but when compared to the typical results of going for the first down on third-and-long, the argument for quick kicking is almost indisputable.

In our offensively productive years of 2000 and 2001, our third-and-long (i.e., 7+ yards to go) conversion rate was around 17%. Coaches and commentators often joke about, "…what is your best third-and-10, -20, -30 play?" In fact, most of the time (83%), no good third-and-long play exists, even if you are fortunate enough to have a pretty productive offense. If you don't have a good offense, this statistic gets worse. In 1999, our third-and-long conversion rate was a pitiful 6%.

In his book *Developing an Offensive Game Plan*, Brian Billick conveys the bleak prospects that anyone faces in a third-and-long situation. He says that a good NFL team should convert 20-25% of third-and-long situations. The difference between my high school team's 17%, which I deemed as "good," and Billick's 20-25% reflects the difference between skill levels of the NFL and high school athletes. Even with a mere three-to-eight percent disparity between the two levels, which straddles the edge of statistical significance, it is safe to say that the odds of converting third-and-long at any level of football are poor.

This factor would seem to make a strong case for quick kicking when you are in third-and-long, and certainly once you begin to approach third-and extra-long situations, because over seventy-five percent of the time, the play that you call will be unsuccessful—especially as the yardage increases. In the very early years of the NFL, moving the ball was so difficult that teams would sometimes quick kick on *first* down. Although the rules favoring today's offenses were not in place, the offenses were saying, in effect, "We don't think we can average the 3.3 yards per play needed in *three* plays to gain a first down." As such, what in the world would make modern-day teams think that they are going to regularly (50% or more) convert the first down from third-

and-15, -20 and -30 yards in *one* play, as many teams regularly attempt. The math suggests this wishful thinking is analogous to cutting your own throat.

Considering a hypothetical situation can provide you with a clearer picture of how this factor can apply. For example, take a fictitious, mid-game, third-and-12 play in a high school game from our own 20-yard line and plot some hypothetically probable results. If we go for it, on an average year, we will get about four yards, leaving us with fourth-and-eight at the 24-yard line—a definite punting situation. We then punt the ball 32 yards, and the return man gets eight yards for a net punt of 24 yards, which leaves the ball on our own 48-yard line. From this point on the field, our opponent has about a one-in-three chance of scoring. They will also have an average drive of around 18 yards, which means the ball will end up on the 30-yard line, a point which most coaches consider "four-down" territory. Given four chances to gain four yards will increase the likelihood that a team will get a first down, because you only need to average 2.5 yards per play instead of 3.3 yards per play. As a result, your opponent's drive has a better chance to continue deeper into your own territory and eventually scoring.

Now, take the same scenario, and instead of going for it on third-and-12, you quick kick. The kick goes 55 yards with no return, which means the ball is on their 25. From this point on the field, their scoring probability is about one-in-eight. In other words, the likelihood of your opponent scoring is about half as much, than if you had gone for it on third-and-12. In addition, you are likely to get the ball back in much more favorable field position by quick kicking.

Instead of having your opponent threatening to score or pin you back deeper, which happened in the "go-for-it-on-third-down" scenario, you are getting the ball back further upfield, and your opponent's threat of scoring is no longer a factor, because they probably punted the ball back to you. By itself, the starting field position of your opponent should be a strong enough motivator for you to quick kick. The difference between starting at their own 25 or your own 48 is 27 yards—a significant field-position advantage for you.

Wouldn't you take a 27-yard play any time you could get it? It is interesting how the yardage a quick kick earns is unappreciated, compared to the yardage a 27-yard pass completion brings. Because one is immediately noticeable, concrete and exciting, the fans cheer. The other one *appears* to be a surrender of sorts, with its advantages being relatively sublime, so it typically elicits shouts of disapproval. Yet, it is clear that the advantage of quick kicking far outweighs its disadvantages. Which scenario paints a prettier picture (not including the sounds of disapproval you'll undoubtedly receive from the stands)?

Not surprisingly, everyone wants to be liked. Some coaches think that their jobs depend on it. A maneuver as "asinine" as regularly quick kicking would surely be unpopular, and may sound the occupational death knell for a coach who is willing to commit to this principle. However, as was previously discussed in this book, some of the most successful coaches (e.g., Al McGuire, Bill Parcels, Tom Osborne, etc.) were individuals who stuck to their principles and strategies despite the "possibility" of disapproval from the fans and media. Keep in mind that these coaches were ultimately smiled upon by history and kept their jobs longer, because they won more games, not because they pleased more fans.

• **Consider using "exotic" formations to prompt an opponent's timeout.** This tactic might be one to consider using before you get into "the push" period, because it will cause your opponent to use timeouts that they would have otherwise used near the end of the game. Technically, this tactic should be used while you are ahead and still in a hurry-up, with the very real possibility that this tactic could be employed in a beneficial way again, while you're in a slowdown at the end of the game. For example, using a swinging-gate or daffy-duck formation will often times cause an opponent to call timeout to decide how to defend it.

After the timeout, you should go back to your conventional offense, and on a series later in the game, try the exotic formation again. Many times, you will be able to force your opponent to call another timeout, because your opponent's players may be unclear concerning how their coach had wanted them to defend it. After all, they did not have any repetitions to practice what their coach had covered with them during the initial timeout. In a very real sense, you are helping to interrupt your opponent's educational chain of events. At the end of the game, when they aren't able to stop the clock anymore, you may find that you are glad that you employed this tactic.

CHAPTER 7

How to Operate
a Hurry-Up Tempo

WARPATH I

Warpath I is our most often used form of hurry-up. A red marker indicates to the team that we are in our second fastest version of hurry-up. It is identified and distinguished from Warpath II, or Red II as we often call it, by "sugar-huddling," instead of no-huddling. Sugar-huddling refers to the fact that we huddle at about six yards, the quarterback quickly reads the signals and then says the play to the team. It was popularized by Sam Wyche, when he was the head coach of the Cincinnati Bengals in the mid '80's. The entire process does not take very long, due in large part to the terminology that we employ in this instance.

As was previously mentioned, we estimate that we can run our offense from over 5000 formations. As a result, reducing our terminology to its lowest terms was of the highest priority when we were revamping our formation package. Among many other reasons, reducing verbage allows us to quickly state the name of the plays we want to run and have them easily understood. We have a system for our snap count, as well, that allows us to not have to say it in the huddle. These principles allow us to run a simple and efficient hurry-up. For example, the terminology for one of our typical plays is quite short, "Ram A 38", and is easily said in a quick, efficient manner.

The reason we have chosen to sugar-huddle, as opposed to no-huddle in Red I, is to prioritize proper communication over the four or five seconds that we save in our no-huddle. Because it is possible that more errors may occur at a faster pace, sugar-huddling enhances our ability to be sure to have everyone "on the same page" in the huddle and to get the play off with six or seven seconds elapsed off the play clock, as opposed to the two seconds we aim for in the no-huddle mode. In Red I, we will also be more apt to use shifts and motions, and sometimes both together, because we are more interested in moving the sticks at this point, than we are about conserving time. Essentially, the biggest differences between Red I and Red II are the huddling and the reading of the signals. In Red I, the quarterback reads the signals from the sideline, and in Red II, the entire team reads these signals.

Although our no-huddle/Red II is effective, we are still working on ways to make the play-calling even more efficient. As was previously discussed, it's the "little things" that separate the champions from the average competitors. As such, this is one area where we think we can be better. Our challenge is to be able to run 100% of our plays in a no-huddle, where the ball is snapped with only two seconds having elapsed from the play clock. Truth be known, very few teams exist that can claim they can do these things with an offensive package of any significant size.

Among the other elements that we use or consider in our Warpath/Red package are the following:

❑ **Offense:**

• **When a timeout is required, call it immediately.**

• **Get out of bounds.** In Red II, this factor is of the utmost importance. In Red I, if the player must stay in bounds to get the first down, he should do so, because at this point in the game, we prioritize possession and moving the ball over stopping the clock.

• **Prefer incompletions to sacks.**

• **Help people off the pile.** If the ballcarrier is tackled in bounds, this step will allow the officials to set the ball faster.

• **Hand the ball to the official.** This step will help the officials to more efficiently set the ball for play.

• **Prefer to run inside the hashes early in the game.** This factor is a lower priority for us, because we are going to run the plays that we think will best move us down the field. On the other hand, all factors being equal, if an inside-the-hash-play and an outside-the-hash-play would be equally effective, we would prefer the inside-the-hash-play.

• **A ballcarrier must get out of bounds or take-a-knee after gaining enough yards to put us in field-goal range, with less than 30 seconds and no timeouts remaining.** You don't want to have him running around and wasting the time that you need to be able to run your field goal team onto the field.

- **Practice using laterals on last play of the game when you're behind by eight points or less.** Even if the player fumbles in his attempt to lateral, there is no risk—you will still lose the game. The worst thing that can happen is that the ballcarrier gets tackled to the ground, and time expires.

- **Use a true Hail Mary.** We call this play "paydirt"—which we got from John Reed. We line up quads to the right and have the receiver on the left, tight to the formation. All of the players run down to a spot in the middle of the end zone, where the tallest, or best leaper of our receivers becomes the center dot on a five die. The four other receivers form the square around him, about three to four yards away. The quarterback aims for the center receiver, and the four other players play for the rebound.

☐ **Defense:**

- **Tackle the ballcarrier out of bounds or to the ground immediately.** This factor will depend upon how much time is left, the field position, and whether or not you are in Red I or Red II. For example, if you are in Red I, and it is earlier in the game, you may be in a position where you can tackle the ballcarrier in bounds for less yards than running him out of bounds.

- **At some point, you must become completely strip-oriented.** If you are trailing late in the game, and your opponents are in imminent danger of running the clock out, your defenders must allow the ballcarrier to make gradual yardage, while trying to strip the ball from him at the same time.

- **Timeouts must be immediate.** As was discussed previously, this situation is one in which you should try to use your timeouts, as opposed to on offense, because you are more in control of how to save time on offense. On defense, your opponent can and should be using the entire play clock, something you would definitely not be doing in Red II. Saving timeouts for offense means you are willing to let the opponents waste more time when *they* are on offense.

- **Consider using a "let-them-score" signal.** The first time we thought of using this tactic was in 1994. We were losing the game 7-6, with about one minute left in the game, and our opponent on our own 15-yard line. Our only chance of winning was to let them score and get the ball back. One of our players, actually suggested it to me on the sidelines. I sent him in the game to tell the defense. Our players looked confused. Frankly, I am not sure they would have executed what we wanted them to do, but we never got the chance to find out, because our opponents wisely knelt out the clock on the next two plays. From that point on, we practiced this particular scenario. The importance of practicing all of the tactics that you might employ in the game will be discussed in a later chapter.

❏ **Special teams:**

• **Punt out of bounds.** The basic case for punting out of bounds is based on the same argument that was advanced earlier in the book regarding kick-offs. Punting out of bounds, however, has the added advantage of not being penalized. One of the most important hidden statistics in the game is net punting average. In fact, we keep track of the percent of punt returns we have versus our opponents.

In 2001, our opponents returned seven of our 47 punts, or 14.9% of them. Our opponents' average punt return yards per game was 3.5. We returned 24 of their 47 punts, or 51.1% of them. Our average punt return yards per game was 15.4, which means we netted almost 12 more yards of field possession in a game than our opponents. While this stat doesn't show up anywhere, it can add up. It is so important, that we will often punt out of bounds in our Hammer I mode, because net field position is more important to us than the few extra ticks off the clock and the risk of a returner taking it back for the score.

In punting out of bounds, you must be able to tolerate one fact that is inevitable: punters will shank punts. In other words, balls that were intended to land out of bounds at the apex of their maximum distance will instead end up being 15-yard shanks on occasion. While this situation is not desirable, it is still better than the alternative.

Coaches and fans seem to get extremely agitated when a punter shanks a 15-yarder. While a 15-yard shanked punt won't exactly make any coach happy either, how is it different than what often happens? For example, a 32-yard punt down the middle of the field that is returned 17 yards ends up with the same net yardage, but people don't seem to get as bent out of shape about this situation as they do about the shanked punt. At least with a shanked punt out of bounds, you can be guaranteed that it won't be returned for a touchdown. In the end, your net punting average will be higher than if you had kicked them all down the middle of the field anyway.

Why no one else seems to subscribe to this theory is perplexing. Perhaps, other coaches find it more desirable to punt the ball deep to one of the opposing team's best open-field runners and see if their coverage men can corral this water-spider of an athlete. All factors considered this tactic does not seem to be a good strategy, relatively speaking. Rather, it is Russian roulette. Eventually you *will* draw the chamber with the bullet.

• **Practice a "sprint field goal".** This tactic is designed for an end-of-the-game, no-timeout scenario, where you must hustle your field goal team onto the field as fast as possible in order to snap the ball with one to three seconds remaining on the game clock. It was previously discussed in more detail in chapter 4.

• **Onside kick.** Sometimes, the results of a bloop or an onside kick are not significantly worse than kicking it deep. This factor is especially true at the youth and junior high levels, where the players can't kick as far, and kicks that go down the middle of the field are often returned a long way, which is why it is not uncommon to see many teams at that level employ this strategy.

• **Use a lateral-oriented return if you are receiving the ball on what will likely be the last play of the game.** This tactic is the old California-Stanford re-run, where the ball was returned by Cal and lateraled several times, ultimately resulting in Cal scoring the winning touchdown on the last play of the game. One of the more memorable moments of this play involved the ballcarrier, who scored the winning touchdown, running into members of the Stanford band who were prematurely celebrating on the field.

ARROW

Arrow is more of an intermediate tempo than a hurry-up tempo, which helps our efforts to avoid leaving extra time on the clock for our opponents. This mode is indicated to our players by using a yellow marker. It is essentially the same as Red II, except the players are told to stay in bounds while not huddling. We have used this only twice in the last three years, but it can be a valuable "arrow" to have in your strategic quiver.

CHAPTER 8

How to Take-a-Knee

This tactic is designed for that point in the game where you want to be able to seal the game or end the half without incident. Too many coaches neglect to spend any time teaching this maneuver. Instead, they wait until game time, at which time, they improvise how this will happen. In our strategic playbook, taking a knee is called our "Victory" mode and is indicated by displaying a white marker to the players. It involves the following factors:

❑ **Offense:**

• **Use the maximum play clock.** In this respect, victory is the same as the Hammer I and II modes. As such, the quarterback will watch the human play clock on the sideline.

• **Use a two tight-end formation with three fullback-types in the backfield.** We have evolved to a different philosophy in this regard. Most conventional take-a-knee personnel alignments involves a "speedster" safety man who is positioned 10- to 15-yards deep, with the thinking being that he could tackle any defender who should happen to scoop up and run with a fumbled snap. Although this situation *could* happen, I have never ever seen it or even heard of it happening. Instead of that alignment, we put three blocking types in who will be able to protect the quarterback longer. As a result, he stays standing longer, and we are able to kill a few precious extra seconds of the clock.

The formation that we employ for taking a knee is like the one we use for a field goal from tight end to tight end, with the guards interlocking their legs with the center's. In the NFL, all linemen should interlock legs, as the rules permit. A fullback will then align one yard behind each tackle. The "safety" man will be moved from the conventional depth of 10-15 yards, up to five yards.

On the snap of the ball, the linemen will step with their inside foot to interlock legs with their respective adjacent lineman. With their outside foot, they will step backwards and inside, similar to a hinge-step. The fullback will momentarily check to see that the snap is successful, before stepping next to the tight end and interlocking his legs with him. Both players will have their backs facing the quarterback. The safety man will also check for the snap, before turning his back to the quarterback as well, leaving the entire team encircling the quarterback with their backs to him. The quarterback, after taking the snap, will step back and use the two-handed Hammer II technique to hold the ball, while getting into a semi-crouched position and swiveling his head to look for any defenders.

With a circle of players around the quarterback, he can remain in relative safety, without worrying about being attacked from an unprotected flank. As such, he can delay taking a knee, while his teammates ward off any would-be tacklers. This step will allow the quarterback to take off more time from the clock, in effect, extending the point at which we can begin to kneel out the clock.

The decision to change to this type of formation was based on the fact that it better addresses the scenarios that actually occur in the game. In 1999, we nearly had our quarterback stripped of the ball, while he was taking a knee in a game that we were winning 20-15. The situation where a defender runs around the offensive linemen and swipes at the quarterback from behind occurs much more often than one where a quarterback actually fumbles the snap. As much, it is a logical strategic step to guard against this "stripping" action, which occurs with all-to-frequent regularity, and still provide some sort of "safety" measure for the rare possibility that the quarterback would drop the snap. All factors considered, it is also a far better approach than what most teams do in having their quarterback immediately take a knee, a tactic that should only be undertaken if you are sure that you won't need to waste the extra time.

As every team should have, we have a take-a-knee chart (Diagram 8-1). This chart takes into account a number of factors, including: opponent's timeouts, what down it is, the amount of time on the clock, the amount of time it takes the official to place the ball (clean-up time), the amount of time it takes us to run the play, and the amount of time we run off the play clock. Although we feel that we can do better in some of the categories than the time we have allotted to that particular category, the chart was developed using less-than-ideal circumstances.

It is also worth noting that the chart includes the equation (written in parentheses) that we employ to calculate how much time will be run off the clock from one play to the next. Having this equation on the sheet in the heat of the moment enables us to observe any deviance the referees might cause from the 11 seconds of "clean-up" time that we have allotted for, as well as our own deviance from the two seconds that we have allotted for ourselves to run the play. As a result, it is possible for us to modify the times on the chart during the game, as appropriate, because of what is happening on the field.

Diagram 8-1. An example of a take-a-knee chart

TAKE-A-KNEE CHART

(23 time to snap the ball+11 clean-up time+2 time to run the play=36 seconds)

OPP. TIMEOUTS>	0	1	2	3
DOWN				
1	1:50	1:16	:42	:08
2	**1:14**	**:40**	**:06**	**:06**
3	:38	:04	:04	:04
4	**:02**	**:02**	**:02**	**:02**

If we are not yet into the take-a-knee period we may be able to use a play that is based on the quarterback-keep-sweep-slide that is advocated by John Reed in his book, *Football Clock Management*. This tactic involves a double tight-end formation, with three fullback/wing players all lined up to one side. When the quarterback gets the snap, he runs backward and toward the sideline, aiming for a depth of 15 yards. When he gets near the sideline, he waits for a defender to get near him and slides to the ground before the defender can touch him. This maneuver will allow him to take extra time off the clock that he would not have been able to waste with the take-a-knee play.

Our keep-sweep-slide (which we refer to as our quarterback-slide play) differs from the one preferred by Reed and others, in that we have our quarterback run the first slide play to his left (if he is right-handed), regardless of what hash the ball is on. Contrary to our philosophy, some individuals recommend that you should always run a quarterback slide to the wide-side of the field. On the other hand, we prefer running the first quarterback-slide play to the quarterback's left, so that if we need to do so on fourth down, we can throw a pass toward a receiver (one of the wings who is not blocking anybody) and out of bounds. Doing this enables us to take an extra four-five seconds off the clock. Using the quarterback slide will allow us to "take-a-knee" at a much earlier point in the game, without running an unnecessarily risky play. The quarterback-slide chart and the minimum yard line you must be on, with worst-case scenarios, are shown in Diagram 8-2.

Diagram 8-2. An example of a quarterback-slide chart

QUARTERBACK-SLIDE CHART

(23 time to snap the ball+15 clean-up time+6 time to run the play=44 seconds)

OPP. TIMEOUTS>		0	1	2	3
DOWN	(YDL)				
1	(50)	2:18	1:40	1:02	:24
2	(35)	1:34	:56	:18	:18
3	(20)	:50	:12	:12	:12
4	(5)	:06	:06	:06	:06

• **Consider using the quarterback-slide play to take a safety if you're ahead by three points or more.** This tactic is why the yard lines are indicated on the chart shown in Diagram 8-2. If you are too close to the end zone, use the slide play until you are out of room, and then consider using a punt formation and snapping the ball past the end line over the punter's head. This maneuver seems to be safer, than having the quarterback take the snap and throw or lateral the ball past the end line, although your willingness to employ this tactic may vary depending upon the confidence you have in certain personnel.

❏ **Defense:**

• **Tackle in bounds and upright.**

• **Do not call timeouts unless absolutely necessary.**

• **All recovered turnovers should be followed by immediately taking a knee.** This mistake can be seen on many occasions in the NFL. The defensive player recovers the fumble at the end of the game and prances around the field weaving in and out of traffic. The only way the team recovering the ball can lose the game at this point is if the player is stripped, and the losing team recovers it to take it in for a touchdown.

• **All fourth-down interception possibilities should be batted to the ground.** This tactic is based on the same rationale as the previous point.

❏ **Special teams:**

• **Take a knee on kick returns.** These kicks should, in theory, usually be onside kicks, but any other bloops, squibs and deep kicks should be knelt down as well.

- **Don't return punts or field goals.** In fact, don't put anybody back for them either. Let them roll.

- **If you must kick off and are ahead by nine points or more with less than 2:00 minutes remaining in the game, consider an onside, a squib to the second tier, or a bloop kick over the front row, or kick out of bounds.** These kicks are less likely to be returned for touchdowns. The kick out of bounds, if your opponent chooses to accept the ball at the 35, is guaranteed to not be returned for a touchdown. Make your opponent take time to score. The *worst* thing that could happen to your team in this situation is having your opponent score in less than 12 seconds; don't kick the ball deep to their *best* athletes and give them the opportunity to do it.

CHAPTER 9

The Push

One of the most difficult determinations a coach will have to make in terms of clock management is at what point his team should either begin to "salt the game away" (when winning) by going into a full-blown slowdown or to "make a run at it" (when losing) by going into a full-blown hurry-up. This situation is the point in the game that I refer to as "the push." It is akin to that time in a basketball game when the losing coach determines that his team's best chance of getting back into the game is by rapidly fouling the opponent on defense and getting quick shots on offense. These steps are all undertaken in an effort to shorten time of possession and give the losers a shot at crawling back into the game. It is also a point that the winning team and losing team should arrive at simultaneously.

Some coaches would argue that if a team is losing, it should use this type of hurry-up at a much earlier point in the game. "If they can score like this, why don't they do it all the time?" the would-be "coaches in the stands" are often heard to quip. As was more thoroughly outlined in Chapter 4, much more compelling reasons for a losing team to be in an all-game slowdown (until the push period) often exist, than can be advanced for trying to play catch-up all game. Although a thorough discussion of those points is not appropriate in this chapter, summarizing those reasons in one simple sentence would conclude that: "an all-game slowdown will sometimes give a team the best possible chance of winning the game, and doing anything else will only serve to widen the scoring gap between that team and its opponent."

In adhering to such a philosophy, the team slowing down from the very beginning will presumably be behind for most of the contest. The rationale behind this philosophy is that the team slowing the game down would be trailing by as few points as possible, when the game nears its conclusion. The major problem with this reasoning is that, if you strictly adhere to this philosophy for the *entire* game you will still lose. You will lose by fewer points, but you will lose. Well, that's a non-proactive way of doing things. Nobody goes into a game hoping to lose "close." At some point in time in the game, you will have to "let off the break," as the slowdown/losing team, and "go for broke".

The same philosophy should hold true for the winning/hurry-up team. At some point in the game, your team will not benefit by increasing the number of possessions, as much as it will by going into a slowdown. In fact, once your team has built a lead significant enough that you feel the opponent's chances of overcoming it are minute; you will only be serving to give the losing team more opportunities to crawl back into the game. So, essentially, at the same time that the losing team should be starting its "push," the winning team should be starting its "anti-push". The winning team will be trying to end the game as soon as possible, while the other team will be trying to extend the game as much as possible, until they regain the lead. At that point, their roles will once again reverse.

Determining the point at which the push should begin is a trickier proposition. In talking to football and basketball coaches alike about when they start the push or anti-push period, none of them could define this point exactly. To a man, they reported that it seems to be more of a "feel thing." Although they do not use an analytical equation to determine when this period starts, as nearly as I can surmise, this starting point seems to be affected by five main factors: 1) time remaining; 2) timeouts remaining; 3) point difference; 4) each team's scoring capabilities; and 5) field position (football only). It is another part of the game that requires your skills as a coach. While a neatly packaged, pre-ordained way of deciding when to "push" does not exist, some general principles do apply.

While I am not at all comfortable with making *the entire process* of determining when the push period should begin "a feel thing," I have attempted to set some general parameters to help determine when this should occur. In this regard, my efforts identify a primary conjecture, which, in turn, has several modifying factors. The resulting conjecture is expressed from the trailing team's point of view from its own 20-yard line and needs only be flip-flopped to apply to the winning team.

☐ **Primary Conjecture:**

A team trailing by one score should plan to need approximately two minutes of game clock to score. This stipulation could vary more or less, depending upon your team's ability to move the ball versus your particular opponent. The process of determining the need for two minutes of clock time is relatively straightforward. For example, if an average play lasts six seconds, and an average play gains four yards, a drive starting 80 yards away from its destination would take 120 seconds or two minutes. Both of these factors will vary—plays will go for more than four yards, but they may also last longer and vice versa.

The validity of this factor was aptly demonstrated by the New England Patriots in Super Bowl XXXVI. Although the Patriots were wisely operating in a mode that slowed the pace of the game down for the majority of the game, when the score was tied with 1:21 left in the game, they went into a hurry-up, because they thought it was the best-case win scenario for them. They ended up moving the ball 53 yards in that time and kicking a field goal as seven seconds of the clock elapsed (two of those seconds rather mysteriously melted away clearly after the officials had signaled the kick as "good").

Although John Madden asserted at the time that the Patriots should have killed the clock and played for overtime, I agreed with the New England staff decision to go for the win then. They felt that their best opportunity for the win would come in the "push" period. In that period they would have one possession and the Rams would be all but guaranteed of having no possessions, unless of course there was to be a turnover. Playing for overtime would have meant that there would be as few as no possessions for the Patriots, because the Rams could have won in sudden death by scoring on their first possession if they had received the ball. At the end of overtime they were playing a "one flip" coin game, which was their best chance of winning. Flipping the coin more times would have meant a greater probability of the heavily favored Rams team winning. If you have any doubt about this, put yourself in the Rams players' shoes and ask what you would prefer: have the Pats try to score in regulation or play for overtime? You would certainly opt to take your team into overtime where your more powerful offense might get the chance to be on offense first.

❏ Modifiers:

• **If your opponents have the ball at their own 20-yard line, and you are behind by one score, add three more minutes to the time you'll need.** This stipulation will vary, depending on your confidence in the ability of your team to stop them. This factor is related to the next point.

The amount of time required to score should decrease or increase in proportion to the confidence you have in the ability of your team to do so. An example of this modifier, expressed from the opposite point of view, happened to us in 2001. We were winning a playoff game 47-39 with 1:47 left on the clock, with the ball on our opponent's 12 yard-line. They had all three of their timeouts remaining. We were into the push period and were wasting as much time as we could. My confidence in our team's ability to stop our opponent, once they got the ball, was not very high. Although we had gained over 520 yards on offense that day, they had gained over 450 themselves. Because of this, I felt that we had to attempt a field goal, which we consequently made and went ahead 50-39.

This strategy involved a tremendous risk that I would normally never have taken. The fastest way for them to get back into the game at that point was to block the kick and take the ball back for a score. But, because I was not confident that we could stop them in the 1:41 that remained after the kick, it seemed like a risk we needed to take. They consequently took the ball down the field 83 yards and scored with :04 left on the clock and missed the subsequent two-point attempt (although they had made two-point attempts earlier in the game).

This situation involved an instance of modifying a standard perception of an opponent's time required to score. I would normally have been content to run a safe play on fourth down in this situation, but because the opponent had had such an inordinate amount of success moving the ball that day I did not want to put us into the "anti-push" mode yet. Doing so, I gauged would not have given us the best chance of winning. Although our opponent scored in 1:37 (very close to the time recommended that you should leave yourself when you need one score), they did not use all three of their timeouts. They also left the clock running for a few extra seconds in several instances in which they should have stopped the clock. At any rate I was still of the opinion that there was a good chance that they could have scored twice, although this was unlikely, and eventually not the case, because we recovered the ensuing onside attempt. As a result, it was not necessary for us to score again.

The point to keep in mind was that I wanted to put our team in the most-likely win scenario. As such, I did not feel that leaving our team with an eight-point advantage was going to give us the most likely win scenario in a game where 95 points had already been scored. In short, we modified our anti-push time by going into it later than we normally would have, because of our opponent's had a strong likelihood of scoring again and doing so quickly.

Conversely, we had a game in 1999 where we were ahead by a score of 21-6 late in the fourth quarter, with the ball on our opponent's five-yard line on fourth-and-goal. In this particular instance, I felt that a two-score advantage was sufficient against an opponent that had managed to score only six points in the game. Their fastest path to winning the game was by blocking a kick and taking it back for the score, as opposed to the 2001 scenario, where I thought our opponent would score anyhow.

In 1999, because I did not think that our opponent was going to be able to move the ball 95 yards for the score, let alone two scores, we ran a safe play. Although we failed to score, our opponent was left with daunting field position. Our strategy was modified, based on what I thought was an opponent's standard scoring ability. In this instance, we modified our push time by going into it sooner than we normally would have, because we thought our opponents had a relatively low likelihood of scoring.

• **For every score you are behind, above and beyond the first one you need, add five minutes onto the initial two minutes you would need if you were behind by one score and had the ball.** If your opponent has the ball, add another three minutes, as previously mentioned. In other words, if you are behind by 14 points and have the ball, you should plan on needing roughly seven minutes. Of course, this time frame might change, depending on the type of field position you have and all of the other variables discussed at the beginning of this chapter. However, if you make certain assumptions, such as the fact that both of your drives will start at your 20-yard line, while the drive your opponent has in between both of your drives will start at its own 20, you should need about seven minutes. This calculation is relatively straightforward. For example, your first drive will require about two minutes. The additional five minutes that you'll need is a function of the amount of time your opponent's ensuing drive will take (another three minutes), combined with your own two minutes, for a total of seven minutes. Three minutes are used as an estimate of the time your opponent's drive will take, instead of two, because they will presumably be trying to waste time. Also, they have the lead, so they have probably had more success in the game, and their chances of gaining a first down or two and keeping the clock running are better.

The combination of you wisely using your timeouts and stopping their drive, along with tackling them out of bounds, are your best means of controlling your opponent's time-wasting efforts. The amount of time required when trailing by two scores can be calculated by the formula that is presented in Diagram 9-1. If you are trailing by three scores, add another five minutes (12 total); if trailing by four scores add ten minutes (17 total). If you are trailing by five scores or more, it is probably time to consider putting in the back-ups, because it is highly unlikely that any team can overcome a five-score deficit, regardless of how much time is left in the game.

Diagram 9-1. A recommended formula for determining how much time you will need, when trailing by two scores.

	2.0	(minutes needed for your first drive)
	3.0	(minutes needed for your opponent's next drive)
+	2.0	(minutes needed for your tying or winning drive)
	7.0	(minutes needed when behind by two scores and you have the ball)

This calculation is quite contrary to how you see most teams manage the clock. It is not unusual to see a team that is behind by two scores not make a concerted, hurry-up effort until four minutes are remaining in the game, almost half the time they will realistically need. While the aforementioned determination of how much time is needed may involve a degree of over-planning, it is not grossly over-exaggerated. Many teams wait until it is too late to make a push to climb back in the game. Always remember that it is better to be left with a little too much time, than not enough time. You can always kill the clock if it looks like you'll score faster than the time you had allotted for scoring.

The converse of this strategy is true as well. With twelve minutes left in the game and a three score lead, the team who is ahead should begin to kill the clock. Even as a blowout favorite, your chances of retaining the lead at this point in the game are very good, especially if you begin trying to end the game as quickly as possible by killing the clock. A perfect example of the application of this factor was the 2001 NFL playoff game that was discussed in chapter 4. The team that led for most of the game could have salted away the victory, but chose instead to run passing plays, which fell incomplete, and left the team that was trailing at the time an open window to tie the game with :27 left. In fact, if the team that was leading had begun an anti-push, or had even attempted to snap the ball with more time having elapsed off the play clock, that game-winning kick would never have happened.

Diagram 9-2 provides a quick reference guide for determining when to start your push/anti-push.

Diagram 9-2. Recommended guidelines for push/anti-push starting times

PUSH/ANTI-PUSH START TIMES CHART				
Scores Behind→→→→	1	2	3	4
Time needed (your ball)	2:00	7:00	12:00	17:00
Time needed (opp. ball)	5:00	10:00	15:00	20:00
(Each timeout can save the trailing team about 40 extra seconds, or 2 minutes w/all 3 left)				

• **The better field position you have, the less time you'll require.** Perhaps, the best way to quantify this factor is for you to have an idea of the number of yards you have to go to score and then to divide that total by the average number of yards per play you think you can average. The more plays you will need, the longer it will take you to score (and vice-versa). This factor is only possible to calculate if you are only one score behind, because you cannot accurately predict your starting field position on your next possession. Just to be safe, you should assume that you will have to go 80 yards on ensuing drives, if you are behind by more than one score.

• **Three timeouts equals two minutes of your opponent's possession time.** As expressed in the chart in Diagram 9-2, one timeout enables you to save about 40 seconds of the clock, assuming that your opponent is shrewd enough to keep the ball in-bounds and keep the clock running during their anti-push phase. Again, these timeouts should be saved for when you are the trailing team and on defense unless you are driving on offense for what you are planning will be your last possession. This tactic will allow you to save the maximum amount of clock time (approximately two minutes), as opposed to using them when you're on offense and have more control of how you'll stop the clock anyhow.

• **If a field goal can win or tie the game for you, use the target yard-line as your figure for how far you have to go, not the goal line.** While this point would seem obvious, arriving at your game-winning or game-tying field goal kick destination too early because you were planning to arrive at the goal line instead will probably mean that you will leave too much time on the clock for your opponent to make a comeback. Incidentally, "too much" time can be defined as little as one second, because that is all that has to be left on the clock to be able to start a play that can result in a touchdown.

• **If you are driving for a score that will be the game-tying or game-winning score, always consider the time left on the play clock, as well as your relative position (yard line) on the field, to determine what tempo to be in.** While the applications of time management in this situation may seem obvious, keep in mind that from a clock-management standpoint, you not only want to score, you also want to leave as little time as possible on the clock after you do score.

Summary Points

The important factor to remember about the push is that as a rule, it is a "feel thing." Some individuals are generally more comfortable with that than others, but it is one of the exciting aspects of coaching. As such, in this regard, you apply a few general guidelines, along with your expert opinion of how the game is unfolding, to determine a strategy that will put your team in the best possible situation to win. If there were hard and fast rules to this strategy, everybody would adopt it, and the game would become the equivalent of watching two computer-coached teams play one another. It is the uncertainty of human error that makes a coach want to see if his strategy is better than the "other guy's." All that being said, it is also foolish to ignore common sense when logic stares you in the face.

CHAPTER 10

The Symbiosis of Offense, Defense and Special Teams

The word symbiosis means an association of mutually interdependent groups. Too often, football coaches treat offense, defense and special teams as if no interdependence exists between them. In fact, many coaches treat offense and defense as if they are two completely different teams and special teams as a minor appendage. In fact, a degree of animosity is present on some football teams between offense and defense that does not exist in any other sport. Undoubtedly, this ill will is due, in part, to the fact that the two phases of football are played with different personnel in a scrimmage-style format, with breaks between every play, as opposed to other sports, which tend to be continuous-play sports where players play both offense and defense.

This attitude of "offense versus defense" is often viewed as playful, harmless ribbing. In reality, the evolution of this counterproductive attitude has developed much more serious consequences. It has grown to the point where the two sides often appear to operate independent of the other side's goals and initiatives. Coaches should keep in mind that this dragon may rear its ugly head in the form of defeats if they don't do something to stop it in their own program. In order to function at a high level of efficiency, both sides must work off the same philosophy, with a common goal in mind, or failure is inevitable. How some coaches have gone this long viewing two interdependent parts of the same system as being mutually exclusive to one another is one of the great mysteries of the sport.

A number of philosophical contradictions within football exist. For example, coaches espouse an aggressive offensive philosophy (e.g., a "run and gun"), that is high-risk and high-reward, while their defense reflects a more conservative "bend, but don't break" philosophy. All factors considered, this dichotomy is absurd. What if your body was operated by independent brains: one for the arms, one for the legs and one for the torso? Parts of your body would being moving all over the place in opposite directions. As a result, getting anything done in a purposeful manner would be purely coincidental and accidental. In the vein, what if I treated my Caravan like a Corvette? I could run it at high speeds and use racing fuel, but in the end, I would probably wreck the car.

Football teams are the same way. You can put a team on the field and run the players in various fashions that are contrary to one another. The team might function in an acceptable way for awhile, but over the course of time, it will not perform the way it was intended and will end up on the scrap heap. Your team is *your* car. As such, if you don't operate the offense, defense and special teams in a philosophically consistent manner, it might be your *job* that ends up on the scarp heap.

It is perplexing to listen to a coach talk about the style of his offense or defense. He talks about one or the other, as if it were a dance move or a trendy skateboard. "We want our defense to be known as a (fill in the blank) _____ type of defense…" and he goes on to explain the defense and how it works. What he often fails to mention is WHY they want to be known as that type of defense. More importantly and more frequently, that coach doesn't explain how it fits in with his program's philosophy.

The philosophy of your offense, defense and special teams has a direct impact on what type of clock management strategy your team employs. Although in a particular year, your team may tend to have qualities that dictate that you operate more in one tempo than another, your X's and O's philosophy should be flexible enough to change from year-to-year and game-to-game to meet the relative strengths of your team in any of the given scenarios listed in chapters 4 and 5.

In this regard, one of the most interesting comments I once heard basketball's Dick Bennett make regarding clock management fell into this area. While Bennett was coaching at Wisconsin, a reporter stated something in his question to the effect that Bennett preferred a slowdown, deliberate style. Bennett briefly interjected that he did not necessarily *prefer* that particular style, and that, if the situation dictated, he would have his teams run an "up-tempo" style. The reporter missed the point and the opportunity to have Bennett expand on this thought, but I am sure that Bennett was referring to the fact that X's and O's philosophy must be flexible enough to adapt to a change in clock-management philosophy. Looking back to when Bennett coached some very successful teams at the University of Wisconsin-Stevens Point, where he coached future NBA great Terry Porter, his teams were known for their fast-paced, run-up-and-down-the-floor style, demonstrating that his system was indeed flexible and situation-based.

In the same vein, football coaches not only need to be able to adapt their X's and O's to any given situation, but also to make sure that their offense, defense, and special teams are on the same page. For instance, an offense that takes chances, with the hope of attaining high rewards (i.e., scoring a lot of points), will probably be a team that stops the clock a lot and runs a high volume of plays per game. To have a defense on the same team that does not take many risks, plays solid schematically, does not vacate many areas when blitzing in order to prevent offenses from exploiting open zones for big gains, and generally seems to have a "bend,-but-don't-break" philosophy to it, would be counter-productive to the team's systematic commitment to winning.

Instead, this team should favor a defense that takes chances and makes big plays. It will unfortunately give up big plays, too, but that should not be a big concern for a team that hangs its hat on scoring a lot of points. The worst thing that this team could do is play a conservative style of defense that regularly allows an opposing offense to meander its way down the field, taking up valuable clock time. It can be even worse than having the opponents score quickly. The fast-paced offense should be banking on the fact that it can outgun its opponents, and any scores by the opponent can be overcome by its own scoring. The offense, and its philosophy, wants as many possessions as possible, and its very own defense is using a philosophy that is designed to accomplish just the opposite. These two units are not working symbiotically for the greater good of the team. It is the responsibility of the head coach to set the philosophy for the game and to be sure that the coordinators are on the same page.

The key point to remember is to avoid allowing yourself or your coordinators to get so hung-up on X's and O's ideas that proper focus on the team's primary goal is obstructed. The goal is to put the team in the most favorable position to win the game. To do anything that hinders this goal would be an example of a typical case of "not seeing the forest for the trees."

Because coordinators often get so caught up in exploring and exploiting an opponent's weaknesses, they sometimes forget that there is a bigger picture. The first flag to which they must be loyal is the one that the head coach sets out. In other words, their schemes must be able to operate as efficiently within the parameters set by the head coach. They must not be allowed to win their own battles and lose the war for the team.

As the head coach, you are the Commander-In-Chief, and they are the Generals who must attack within the system. Developing an offensive or defensive identity because a coordinator wants his offense or defense to be known as "X" is planning without a long-term purpose. As a rule, it is also a recipe for disaster.

Remember that if you want your football team to be a football *program*, it has to work together. The offense, defense and special teams are all part of a complex system. The actions of one will have a direct impact on the other parts and, more importantly, on the whole team. If all three parts are pulling in the same direction, the net result will be a synergistic use of forces, rather than a conflicted set of independent anomalies.

CHAPTER 11

How to Practice Clock Management

Now that you know how clock management can be of great benefit in helping you win more football games, if you are like most coaches, you are probably mentally resisting the urge to make it a full-fledged part of your program. The cause of your anxiety likely has something to do with the attitude, "I don't have the time to do this type of stuff in practice."

Two plausible responses can be advanced concerning such an attitude. First, if something is important enough for you to win more games, it is important enough for you to practice. If you think that clock management truly is a "little" thing, and you feel that you must devote the precious practice time you have to the "big" things, ask yourself what your players would say if they knew you chose to skip the little things that could help your team win more games. Second, practicing clock-management tactics does not take time away from practice. As you will see, it actually saves time. We practice clock management as much as anybody, and we never had a single practice go longer than two hours in the past three years.

Before you practice clock management, you must take steps to have your staff fully understand the rationale for sound clock management. Your first step, if possible, should be to require all of the coaches on your staff to read this book. Such an undertaking should lead to some excellent discussion of how clock management can benefit your program. It will also get everyone on the same page, collectively stressing the importance of clock management. From there, the principles and concepts attendant to sound clock management should be much easier to impart to your players.

We begin teaching clock management to our team on the first day of practice. In the break between our first and second practice, we meet with our players in the classroom. In addition to installing some of the plays we will be practicing once we get on the field, we will introduce our red/hurry-up mode. By doing this, we are able to get a maximum amount of repetitions when we get into the team period, because our team mode is run in no-huddle more than 98% of the time.

On the *first day* of practice, we install and practice one of the major tempos in clock management. We don't need to take time out of practice to practice this tempo; *it is practice*. In fact, because we install and run at a hurry-up pace everyday, we are getting more repetitions of what coaches normally think of as "the big stuff," as previously discussed. As a result, by using clock management we are actually *saving* time in practice, instead of *taking* time in practice to specifically work on clock management.

Incidentally, because such a small difference exists between our Yellow mode and our Red mode, we install these modes on the first day of practice as well. It does not take very long to get the ballcarriers accustomed to the idea, for example, that in Yellow, they must stay in-bounds instead of running out of bounds.

Two days later, we install the Green/Hammer mode. A 15-minute investment in a meeting, and the bare-bones installation is done. It does not take much time to practice the basics of this mode. Aside from huddling, (which takes a little more time and teaching the quarterback to look at the human play clock on the sideline), practicing this mode does not take more time. Part of how we save time practicing this mode is by simulating to the quarterback that the 25-second clock has already run down, as opposed to waiting the entire time, which would include the time it takes the referee to place the ball, etc.

During the week of our first game, we practice our White mode. Because this mode and the Hammer mode share many common characteristics, it does not take the players very long to catch on to the White mode. It takes approximately 15 minutes to install White and to be ready to run it in the game. The point to keep in mind is that with as little as 15 minutes of instruction, we are able to incorporate this into our game plan with little or no confusion concerning player assignments or responsibilities.

All of the basics of our dictated tempo are installed well before two-a-day practices are over. In fact, as soon as we have installed a particular mode, for example Red, we begin scripting scenarios for the very next practice in that mode in order to get the players thinking about the nuances of that mode. This step does not take any time away from practice either, because it is all done "on the fly," as it would happen in a game, so the players begin to think about it as a natural part of the game.

In addition, we have found that the players need very few repetitions on a regular basis of any parts of the dictated tempo to keep their understanding of a particular mode fresh in their heads. It is not the same as learning a physical skill, such as punting, that can require thousands of repetitions to master. Instead, after a few repetitions, you'll find that most players have mastered the mode and will become bored if you make them go through *all* of the tiniest details concerning that mode, over and over again. As a rule, they will have the details of how to properly execute a dictated tempo down pat. On the other hand, we review selected parts of a particular tempo from time to time, as some form of clock management is always discussed and/or reviewed in every practice.

The use of clock management becomes second nature to our players. Their understanding and acceptance of sound clock management is truly amazing. For example, on almost every Monday, at least one player, sometimes many, will approach me and say, "Coach did you see that game on TV yesterday, where they should have..." and go on to explain a facet of clock mismanagement that they observed in the game. They will also regale me with stories of how they beat one of their buddies in a video football game by using proper clock management.

On one occasion, I went to watch a local playoff game with some other coaches. Some of our players were in attendance at the game and ended up watching part of the game with us. As the game progressed, the players were talking amongst themselves about the flaws in clock management that were occurring during the game. They would then lean over and see if I concurred with them, whereupon we ended up having discussions about it. One of the other coaches I was with started to laugh about our situation. One of the coaches then expressed his opinion of the situation by stating, "Your kids are thinking about clock management strategy, and mine are probably deciding what kind of pizza they want to order."

Another example of how clock management becomes engrained in our player's thinking happened while we were in the weight room one summer evening. Another coach who was about to begin his first season coaching with us was there, too. We were talking about clock management and how we *do* have enough time to practice this stuff. I called the first player I saw over and asked him if he knew what a Cal-Stanford kick return was. Without any hesitation, he explained what it was and the appropriate situation for the proper application.

It had easily been nine months since we had practiced the play, and when we did, we only did it four times. FOUR repetitions, nine months ago, and he knew in an instant what it was and everyone's responsibility. How often do you suppose I would have to review this? This reason reflects exactly why practicing clock management does not take a significant amount of time to practice. As previously discussed, it probably even saves time to practice it.

Players tend to retain the mental aspects of the game, in much the same way that you, as a coach, retain the X's and O's *ideas* that you've heard at a clinic. The first time you hear a particular idea, you may require a bit of extra time to understand its rationale. However, by the third or fourth time you're exposed to a particular notion, your confidence in understanding the concepts inherent in that idea will have grown considerably. Even if you decide to not use the particular scheme being discussed, you will probably retain many of the base ideas attendant to that scheme for years to come. Certainly, with occasional exposure, you will develop a meaningful degree of confidence in your understanding of the base concepts.

Another extremely important element of practicing clock management relates to turnovers. Our players are taught to protect the ball on offense and cause and recover turnovers on defense. There are too many coaches who preach the importance of not turning the ball over, but don't follow through on how to help their players in this regard. They don't *coach* players on how to not turn the ball over; they just yell at them when they do.

No matter how loudly you yell "hang on to the ball!" at a player, it does not really help him learn how to not fumble the ball. This admonition must be followed-up with specific action. In this regard, there are a number of actions we take to help our players achieve the goal of not turning the ball over. On the defensive side of the ball, as well, although coaches have been known to shout, "we need a take-away," they have never spent a single minute practicing how to do this.

Offensively, the first, and probably most important, way to get a player to focus on not fumbling the ball or throwing an interception is to bench him. Nothing speaks to a player's heart like riding the pine. I once did this to a very good running back and one of my all-time favorite players. I knew he would do anything I asked him to do. This particular player was a diligent worker and an excellent leader (only the second two-year captain I ever had). He was the co-valedictorian of his class and was extremely coachable. He was a coach's dream, except for one thing—he had a fumbling problem.

I knew he wanted to do what I told him to do, I knew he understood what I wanted him to do, and I knew he understood how significant a part of the game turnovers were. I also knew that if I couldn't get a player with this particular player's intangibles to learn how to hang on to the ball, I was not the coach that I wanted to be or should be.

The first action I took in this regard was to stop giving him the ball (a benching of sorts). In the next two games, *he* carried the ball one time. He did eventually carry the ball and fumble less during the remainder of the season, but what happened with the tailback who replaced him, was equally interesting. This particular player was told that he would now be getting the lion's share of the carries, because he had not fumbled. He went on to carry the ball over 200 times that season before he lost his first fumble. In fact, he ended the year with only one fumble in 213 carries. As a consequence, we were +7 in our giveaway/takeaway ratio that year and ended the regular season at 7-2, before losing in the first round of the playoffs. *Coaching point:* Give more than lip service to your priorities or the players won't prioritize them the same way you do. Nothing speaks louder than playing time.

Getting back to the aforementioned player who had a problem with fumbling. We moved him to fullback, and we also worked harder with the entire team on the techniques of ball security. That player ended up carrying the ball the following year as a fullback in a tailback-oriented offense 159 times for 915 yards and only fumbled once. I firmly believe that adjusting his playing time accordingly, along with coaching the technique better, was the prime reason that this player learned to not fumble the ball, which leads into the second step we take to help ensure ball security—how to properly carry the ball.

First, we teach our players how to properly carry the ball with one arm. We describe this technique as "high and tight." We liken the way the ballcarriers carry the ball to the way a guitar strap or machine gun ammunition belt would ride over your shoulder. The arm should be in the middle of the chest and quite high, so that the coach (or would-be defender) cannot see the ball from behind at all. Additionally, the elbow of that arm should pinch down toward the player's abdomen so the ball cannot be knocked down through the "arm hole" that would otherwise be present. As he runs, the arm that carries the ball should not rock up and down at all, regardless of the ballcarrier's proximity to any defender or his position on the field. It should remain stationary, as if the ball were nailed through his chest with a 16-penny spike. This technique will undoubtedly slow the carrier to a degree, but we feel it is more than worth the pay-off of not having a turnover.

During our conditioning period, the ball bags are emptied, and the players who carry the ball the most are given a ball, until all of the balls are distributed. The players must go through the entire conditioning period carrying the ball as described. This is accompanied by the constant swatting and strip-attempts of coaches' hands as players run by. As a result of the players' and coaches' persistence in this matter, we have reaped tremendous benefits. Over the past two seasons, our leading tailbacks have carried the ball 213 and 288 times, respectively, for a total of 501 carries and 3376 yards. Over that time period, there has only been *one fumble* between the two backs combined, The one player who has not fumbled in two years of playing regularly still has his senior season left to play.

When we go into our Hammer II mode the technique that we require our backs to use when carrying the ball is modified slightly. The ballcarrier will still carry the ball in a high-and-tight manner, but he will now put his other hand on the ball as well. This method is not the "two-hands-on-the-football" technique that is sometimes taught elsewhere, where the ballcarrier folds one arm over the top of the ball and the other arm under the ball. Our experience with that technique has not been good. We have found that this technique is conducive to turnovers, especially if the ballcarrier is knocked off his feet. Many backs, in an effort to break their fall, will allow their folded arms to come forward and away from their bodies, leaving the ball susceptible to falling out from underneath.

We have modified the two-handed technique our backs use in Hammer II to be more of a "baby-carrying" position with the off-hand. In other words, the arm that is not carrying the ball in the high-and-tight position will be placed on the ball on the underside of the ball, or the side of the ball that is exposed to the ground. When backs are knocked off their feet while carrying the ball this way, their bottom hand serves to keep the ball from falling out the bottom, while still giving the back an elbow to use as a shield in the urge to break his fall. We have found this technique to be much more effective in preventing turnovers.

This technique is particularly applicable in Hammer II—a time that merits a high enough priority to tell our backs, "get two hands on the ball!" Players carrying the ball in Hammer II are instructed to have two hands on the ball, regardless of where they are on the field or how close they are to any defender. Every ballcarrier must have two hands on the ball *at all times*. Any player who does otherwise finds himself standing next to me on the next play.

We also have our quarterbacks and centers regularly work on their exchanges. We require each group to get a minimum of 20 perfect snaps before and after each practice. We demand that these be done with the highest level of intensity and exertion and with a specific play in mind. This requirement helps accurately simulate actual game-time conditions. As such, players are practicing at a level close to "real game." Allowing players to practice this skill in a lackadaisical manner could be devastating, and would actually be worse than if they hadn't practice exchanges at all. Players practicing at a less-than-high level of intensity will be engraining the wrong tempo and intensity into their muscle memory. As a result, they will probably fumble more in the game because of their bad practice repetitions.

Defensively, we try to encourage our players to force and recover turnovers. Everyday, we begin practice with some type of ballhawk drill, which lasts about seven minutes. In addition to serving as an excellent, football-specific warm-up, it engrains in the players' minds and muscle memory the importance and technique related to this highly prioritized facet of the game. We have about a dozen different ballhawking drills, which focus on stripping the ball and/or recovering the ball in an array of different situations. We have won at least three games in the past two years, where a strip and recovery in a critical situation was the difference in the game.

It is difficult to say exactly how many games we won because we had a positive turnover ratio, but a number of statistics point to the fact that this factor definitely has a major impact on the outcome of the game. With regard to this factor, one study that

I conducted of a high school's 31 year history of football found that 86% of the time when the team had a positive turnover ratio, the team had a winning record that year.

Another statistic I currently keep track of and post for our players is the game-by-game correlation between a positive turnover ratio and winning. From 1999 through 2002, our team is 18-2 (.900), when we have a positive turnover ratio for the game. On the other hand, we are 1-12 (.077), when it's negative, and 3-5 (.376), when we are even. This evidence is enough for me, and the reason why we make such a big deal out of turnovers and how we promote ball control on offense and ballhawking on defense.

On one occasion, one of our defensive backs was closing in to make a tackle on a running back, who had broken through the line and was on the five-yard line about to score. The running back's momentum would surely have carried himself and the defender into the end zone for the score, but the defensive back executed the "windmill punch," jarring the ball lose off the running back's knee. Whereupon, the ball went out the back of the end zone for a touchback. We went on to win that game 7-6.

After the game, a number of people came up to me and said, "What a play the DB made, you don't teach a kid that!" I replied, "The hell we don't; we do it at the start of every practice." The key point that should be remembered in this regard is that the repetitions you give a player are more likely to be transferred into a real game than if you had not practiced a particular skill at all. Although our defensive back had a real knack for this skill, having finished second and third in 2000 and 2001, respectively, in our "ballhawk" competition, he admitted to me that the strip was something he didn't really even think about—it just happened. This is presumably a result of the countless repetitions he had in practice.

Yet another way we encourage stripping-the-ball skills, as was alluded to in the previous paragraph, is to have a ballhawk competition each year. Players are awarded points for every single way they contribute to actions related to ballhawk principles. These points are the basis for their helmet awards, and are the only reason we give any helmet award. Because it is our only helmet award, it emphasizes its importance to the player, and, more importantly, it is something the player can *do something* about.

Inexplicably, some coaches give awards for everything under the sun. This philosophy can really confuse the players as to what is *really* important to their coaches. Other coaches confer awards for feats I know the players aren't thinking about during the game. Giving the team an award because they rushed for 5.0 yards/carry is a nice gesture, but whether this transfers to what the player is doing on the field is highly doubtful. At best, it is problematic that a player will line up and concentrate on the idea that he is going to block or hand the ball off or whatever well enough to get his team at least five yards.

You could question whether you really want your players thinking about this type of statistic anyhow. So, why do coaches give such awards? It seems as though goals of this type are more appropriate for the coaching staff to have, than for the players to think about. Awards should be used to motivate players to want to do something. Too many awards that coaches give do not focus on a specific action a player can take to help his team. Rather, they focus on ideas. The key point is that players can line up and concentrate on having a good quarterback/center exchange, for for example, or some other skills related to ballhawking. Such focal points are in direct contrast to some of the inappropriate goals that many coaches advocate—pointless objectives don't motivate the players to any particular action on the field, during the game. Instead many of those goals get players to admire something they did not even know they did until after the game.

Furthermore, the only statistics that are put up on our bulletin board are related to ballhawking and turnovers. This step enables the players to focus on what you deem most important as opposed to the "glory" statistics to which many players are drawn. Every Monday, when the players come into the locker room, the first thing they look at is what is happening with the ballhawk and turnover charts. Diagrams 11-1 through 11-3 illustrate examples of the stats that we hung up in our locker room during the 2001.

In addition, we only give out three team awards at the end of the year. One of them is the ballhawk award. The other two are "Strength and Conditioning" and "Heart of a Warrior" (an award that is bestowed on the player who best embodies the program's pillars of hustle, heart and humility). Making everybody feel special is not what we are all about. We are about producing desired effects. By rewarding a select few, the players are better tuned in to what the coaching staff deems most important.

If you want your team to be good in the turnover department, you better do more than just being vocal about it. While some turnovers truly are bad luck, a good deal of them are preventable. The key point in this regard is to be productive in preventing turnovers. Don't put your team in the position of feeling like you are rolling the dice, hoping to avoid the "turnover bug" as if you have no role in their occurrences. You must take the time to make avoiding turnovers on offense and creating them on defense an important aspect of your program.

Diagram 11-1. Giveaway/takeaway stats for the 2001 season

GIVEAWAY/TAKEAWAY STATS:

<u>OC</u>
Them 4 (I/3F)
<u>Us 1(F)</u>
Game: +3
Result: Lost
Year: +3

<u>FR</u>
Them 2 (I/F)
<u>Us 0</u>
Game: +2
Result: Won
Year: +5

<u>RP</u>
Them 2 (2F)
<u>Us 2 (2F)</u>
Game: Even
Result: Won
Year: +5

<u>KT</u>
Them 1 (F)
<u>Us 2 (2I)</u>
Game: -1
Result: Lost
Year: +4

<u>KB</u>
Them 0
<u>Us 0</u>
Game: Even
Result: Won
Year:+4

<u>RH</u>
Them 1 (I)
<u>Us 3 (1I/2F)</u>
Game: -2
Result: Lost
Year: +2

<u>SM</u>
Them 0
<u>Us 0</u>
Game: Even
Result: Won
Year: +2

<u>BT</u>
Them 2 (I/F)
<u>Us 0</u>
Game: +2
Result: Won
Year: +4

<u>RC</u>
Them 3 (I/2F)
<u>Us 0</u>
Game: +3
Result: Won
Year: +7

<u>MR</u>
Them 2 (I/F)
<u>Us 0</u>
Game: +2
Result: Won
Year: +9

<u>MQ</u>
Them 3 (I/2F)
<u>Us 1 (I)</u>
Game: +2
Result: Won
Year: +11

<u>KT</u>
Them 0
<u>Us 3 (1I/2F)</u>
Game: -2
Result: Lost
Year: +2

	2001	Since 1999	
W/L RECORD WITH "+" TURNOVER RATIO:	5-1	13-2	.867%
W/L RECORD WITH "-" TURNOVER RATIO:	0-3	1-8	.111
W/L RECORD WITH "EVEN" TURNOVER RATIO:	3-0	3-4	.429

Diagram 11-2. Team ballhawk stats, by category

Rushing (ballcarrier is stripped, drops handoff, drops ball):

Fumbles

Them:	Fumble/attempt:	(24 fumbles/411attempts)	1 fumble every 15.2 carries
Us:	Fumble/attempt:	(8 fumbles/605 attempts)	1 fumble every 75.6 carries

Fumbles lost

Them:	Fumbles lost/attempt:	(12 fumbles lost/411 attempts)	1 fumble lost every 34.3 carries
Us:	Fumbles lost/attempt:	(4 fumbles lost/605 attempts)	1 fumble lost every 151.3 carries

Passing:

Them:	Int/pass attempt:	(7 Interceptions/217 attempts)	1 interception every 31.0 pass attempts
Us:	Int/pass attempt:	(5 Interceptions/93 attempts)	1 interception every 18.6 pass attempts

QB/Center exchanges:

Fumbles

Them:	9	(9 fumbles/628 offensive plays)	1 fumbled snap every 69.8 plays
Us:	1	(1 fumble/698 offensive plays)	1 fumbled snap every 698 plays

Fumbles lost

Them:	1	(1 fumbled snap lost)	1 fumbled snap lost every 628 offensive plays
Us:	0	(0 fumbled snaps lost)	-

Special teams:

Fumbles lost

Them:	0	(0 fumbles/47 special teams plays)	-
Us:	2	(2 fumbles/56 special teams plays)	1 fumble every 28 special teams plays

Overall:

Them:	7 Int's + 13 fumbles = 20 turnovers in 675 total plays	1 turnover every 33.8 plays
Us:	5 Int's + 6 fumbles =11 turnovers in 754 total plays	1 turnover every 68.5 plays

Diagram 11-3. Player-by-player ballhawk standings for the 2001 season

2001 MUSKEGO WARRIORS
BALLHAWK STANDINGS

OPP.	OC	FR	RP	KT	KB	RH	SM	BT	RC	MR	MQ	KT	Total
Petfalski	2	1	1	1	4*	6	7*	6*	5	3	9	4	49
Somodi	4	3*	1	1	4	1	3	4*	4	2	7	3	37
Fitz	2	1	1	1	2	1	4	5*	3		13**	3	36
Hoeffler	3	5	4	1	3	1	2	3	1	5	4	3	35
Smith	2	3	1	1	2	1	1	2	4	1	3	1	22
Knudsen	2	1	5*	2	1			1	2	1	4		19
Augustine		1	2*		3			3	1		7	1	18
Larsen	6	5	1		1						2		15
Blawat								4	4		4	1	13
LeMaster	4	2	1						4				11
Kucharas	1	1		1	2			1	3		2		11
Hagen		1						1	2	1	2		8
Meinen		1						1	1		2		6
Moore	1		1			1			1		1	2	8
Plautz	4				1								5
Wooten			1	1			1						3
Azarian			1				1	1					3
Murphy								1	2				3
Nelson	1					1							2
Schmidt		2											2
Illies								2					2
Hansen					1						1		2
Martin					1					1			2
Croak										1	1	1	3
Stephens		1											1
Miller				1									1
Roozen			1										1
Blosky					1								1
Albert					1								1
Rickard						1							1
Riemer							1						1
Wegner							1						1
Goodson									1				1

*indicates game-saving/game-winning/game-breaking ballhawk effort

EPILOGUE

I have come a long way in my understanding of the ramifications of football clock management. While understanding it can initially be a somewhat complex undertaking, its applications are relatively simple. They are so simple, and the benefits so great, that you would be remiss, as a coach, in not making sound clock management the backbone of the way your program operates. One of the most dismaying factors about clock management in football is that too few coaches have an in-depth understanding of this critical component. On the other hand, one of the most exciting things about this situation is, if you are motivated to implement clock management in your program, you will have a meaningful edge over nearly everybody else.

All factors considered, you are virtually getting in on the ground floor of a powerful and underestimated tool for success. Clock management is one of football's most well kept secrets. It is what every coach says he is looking for, "What is that one element that will give me even a little bit of an advantage over our opponent?"

We all know that nothing can replace athletes who know how to block and tackle—which is why we spend much of our time trying to improve our respective teams in these areas. However, when all of the players are in place on your team, and all of the blocking and tackling drills have been taught, and your scheme versus their scheme has been incorporated into your game-plan protector sheet, don't forget to give your team that "little extra edge"—the "winning edge" that sound clock management will provide.

ABOUT THE AUTHOR

John Sterner is the head football coach at Muskego High School (Muskego, WI), a position he has held since 1999. His 2000, 2001, and 2002 teams have advanced to the Wisconsin state playoffs, while breaking several school records in scoring, offense, and rushing yardage. His 2001 team made it to the WIAA division I quarterfinals, despite having the second lowest enrollment in the state's largest division. At the conclusion of the 2000 season, he received several "Coach of the Year" honors, and was selected to coach for the south squad in the Wisconsin all-star Shrine Game. His teams have been noted for their success in employing a multiple-formation zone offense and their disciplined application of clock-management strategies. He has written and spoken on numerous football topics and has most recently co-authored a book on practice organization.

As a collegiate athlete, John was a two-sport standout in track and football at the University of Wisconsin-Whitewater. In track, he became a two-time all-American pole vaulter, while in football he was a three-year starter at wide receiver, team MVP, and co-captain. His stints as an assistant football coach have included the University of Wisconsin-Whitewater, where he coached wide receivers, including all-Americans Paul Jones and Anthony Talton, the latter of whom received several NFL tryouts. Other coaching stops have included Waukesha Catholic Memorial HS, and Marquette University HS, where he coached outside linebackers under the state's all-time winningest coach, Dick Basham, winning the state championship in 1997. He has also served as the head football coach at Eudora HS (KS) and Beloit Turner HS (WI).

John holds degrees in English and health, as well as a master of science degree in curriculum and instruction. He currently teaches English at Muskego High School, in addition to his head coaching responsibilities with the Warriors' gridiron team. He and his wife, Sue, reside in Wind Lake, Wisconsin, with their daughter, Keeley, and son, Jack.